HUMAN ECOLOGY

HUMAN ECOLOGY

A Theoretical Essay

Amos H. Hawley

The University of Chicago Press
Chicago • London

To Steve, Maggie, Susie, and Patty

The University of Chicago Press, Chicago 60637
The University of Chicago Press, Ltd., London
© 1986 by The University of Chicago
All rights reserved. Published 1986
Printed in the United States of America

01 00 99 98 97 96 95 94 93 92   3 4 5 6 7 8

Library of Congress Cataloging-in-Publication Data

Hawley, Amos Henry.
  Human ecology.

  Bibliography: p.
  Includes index.
  1. Human ecology. I. Title.
GF21.H38   1986   304.2   86-7077
ISBN 0-226-31984-9 (pbk.)

Contents

v

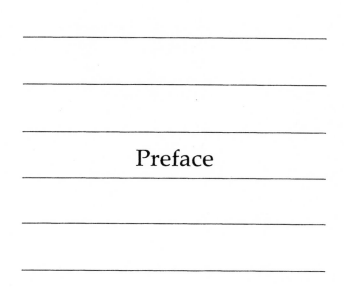

Preface

For some years I have speculated on the feasibility of a unified theory of human ecology. It has seemed to me that, if one could identify the necessary assumptions, it would be possible to derive a set of propositions that would constitute at least the framework of a coherent and parsimonious theory. Furthermore, if this were done properly, causal relations not directly specified in the propositions could be derived by deductions from those propositions. I wish I could say that in this volume that challenge has been met and overcome. But any such claim would be presumptuous. The most I dare say is that I have made a little progress toward that ambitious objective. Perhaps others will be encouraged to try to complete the task.

As a theoretical exegesis the essay has relatively little empirical content. I have included only enough material from research reports to suggest that the hypotheses are at least plausible. That, of course, does not do justice to the huge amount of research literature bearing upon many of the points made in the text. For that omission I ask forgiveness. I like to think, however, that the hypotheses set forth lend themselves to operational treatment.

Persons who have read earlier publications of mine will find much that is familiar in this volume. Indeed I have plagiarized myself without restraint. I have felt justified in doing so because my intention in preparing this essay has been to bring together in an orderly statement a number of interrelated ideas. But this is not to say that there is nothing new in the essay. I have carried more than a few earlier thoughts two or three steps beyond their initial formulations, and I have tried to fill lacunae that had been left unattended in past writings.

I would very much like to acknowledge the contributions others have made to this work. But I do not know how to do that in the fullness it merits. During nearly forty years of associations with graduate students and colleagues I have been the beneficiary of so many criticisms, counterproposals, and extensions of ideas, as many subtle and inadvertent as direct and explicit, that I am unable to sort them out in order to give credit where it is due. I would be remiss, however, were I to fail entirely in this matter. My indebtedness to the "Chicago School," especially to R. E. Park, E. W. Burgess, and R. D. McKenzie, is obvious. Among the many others to whom I feel obligated are Thelma Batten, Donald Bogue, Dudley Duncan, Ronald Freedman, Arthur Hinman, Michael Irwin, Michael Kennedy, Werner Landecker, Gerhard Lenski, Krishnan Namboodiri, Lee Schnore, David Smith, John Wardwell, Everett Wilson, and Basil Zimmer. There are still others too numerous to mention; they fill the reference list at the end of the volume.

Finally, I must acknowledge my very great debt to the sociology department of the University of North Carolina at Chapel Hill for granting me access to its resources. I am especially grateful to Anna Tyndall, Priscilla McFarland, and Priscilla Preston for their assistance in the preparation of the manuscript.

1

Introduction

Ecology Defined

Ecology is commonly defined as the study of the relation of organisms to their environment. While this is useful as a generic statement, it begs for amplification. There are differences in how we define the major parameters and how we treat the relation between the parameters. The differences range from concerns with very specific environmental features to environment quite broadly conceived, from organisms treated individually (autecology) to organisms regarded as collectivities (synecology), and from ontogenetic to phylogenetic perspectives.

From General to Human Ecology

The position of human ecology in this context was determined primarily by the point of view cultivated initially by sociologists, particularly to account for certain aspects of American cities in the first quarter of the nineteenth century (Park and Burgess 1921; Park 1925, 1936a; Burgess 1925; McKenzie 1924, 1926). Cities of that period were experiencing rapid and turbulent growth. Large-scale influxes of ethnically diverse populations, uncontrolled competition for space, rapid obsolescence of physical structures, and almost continuous redistribution of land uses presented a superficial picture of chaos. To find order in the welter of change presented a challenge that could be met only in a macroscopic view of the phenomenon as a whole. A useful perspective was suggested by the then-current work of plant ecologists. They (Clements 1916; Clements and Shelford 1939) had observed that the flora of an area comprise an assemblage of species engaged in complementary uses of the habitat. The community, as the association of species is characterized, exhibits a clear temporal and spatial pattern that is expressive of a functional order. A dominant species controls the light, water, and soil conditions in the area, and subdominants fit themselves into locations that enable them to utilize diurnal and seasonal variations in light while drawing upon, and assisting in the maintenance of, soil and water resources. The plant community acquires its organization in a process described as succession—an orderly sequence of invasions and displacements culminating in a climax or equilibrium state (Odum 1969).

Many of the features of the plant community seem to have analogies in the urban community. The notions of an association of species joined in a division of labor and thereby forming a distinguishable adaptive unit, of dominance diminishing on a gradient with distance from a center of influence, and of a naturalistic development moving through a sequence of stages appeared to be transferable with slight modifications to the urban community. Although these ideas were subsequently elaborated with analogies from animal ecology and from physiology, the model constructed by the early human ecologists from these borrowings retained the imprint of the plant community. The persistence of that influence was doubtlessly due to the fact that both plant and human communities exhibited highly visible spatial patterns. Sociologists seized upon the spatial dimension of human interrelations as the sine qua non of human ecology and proceeded to produce a great volume of field research on the spatial pattern of the city and the correlates of that pattern. So confined to that preoccupation were the early researchers that human ecology came ineluctably to be regarded as a study of spatial distributions. Indeed, Robert Park (1929) went so far as to suggest that sociology would become scientific to the extent that social relations could be reduced to measures of distance.

But there is another and more fruitful lesson to be learned

from the work of plant and animal ecologists: a workable relationship with the environment is achieved not by individuals or even species acting independently, but by their acting in concert through an organization of their diverse capabilities, thereby constituting a communal system. Adaptation is seen as a collective rather than as an individual process. What is necessary for lower forms of life is even more compelling for human beings, for the latter possess far more generalized anatomical and physiological equipment. It became evident, therefore, that an understanding of the relationship of human beings to environment requires a full knowledge of the human social system. Until that is developed, an appreciation of the character of environmental influence cannot advance beyond a rudimentary level.

Accordingly, the focus of human ecology shifted to a concern with the ways in which human populations organize in order to maintain themselves in given environments, thus relegating spatial analysis to a minor though still useful position in the discipline. Nor did it eliminate an interest in the city. The city is a conspicuous example of a system of relationships among differentiated activities by means of which a population is able to occupy a unit of territory. It is, however, one of a class of such systems. All members of the class fall within the purview of human ecology. Quite clearly, therefore, human ecology is a sociological concern. This will become more apparent as I examine the elements of the theory.

The mutualism between bioecology and human ecology, present from the beginning, has abated somewhat in recent years.[1] The parent discipline drew a number of its initial concepts, such as community, dominance, and succession, from usages familiar to social scientists. More recently a very active concern known as population ecology has developed in bioecology; it involves applying demographic techniques to studies of animal populations. The Malthusian model, the origins of which lie in the early interactions of biological with social thought, occupies a prominent position in population ecology studies.

As already noted, human ecology borrowed extensively from the lexicons of plant and animal ecologies in its formative years. Many of the concepts so obtained are still current in the theoretical writings of human ecologists. The most important contribution, however, is the perspective of collective life as an adaptive process consisting of an interaction of environment, population, and organization. Out of that process emerges the ecosystem, a concept that serves as a common denominator for bioecology and human ecology.

Fundamental as the ecosystem concept seems, it is not used consistently by bioecologists. For Dice (1952, 21) and Emmel (1973, 3) the term pertains to a community of organisms together with their habitat. Slobodkin (1962, 9) limits the term to community, while Margalef (1968, 4) defines *ecosystem* as a network of interacting organisms. Although neither Clements and Shelford (1939, 21–25) nor the Buchsbaums (1957, 58–83) use the term, both address their works to the community in much the same sense used by Slobodkin and Margalef. Nevertheless, there appears to be consensus that at a minimum *ecosystem* denotes a network of interdependences that functions as an adaptive mechanism. Such a definition is congenial with the needs of human ecology. That leaves untouched a number of questions concerning, for example, the degree of closure of the system, the nature of the developmental process, the characters of the units of organization, and the treatment of equilibrium. These and other issues will be discussed in later paragraphs.

Defined as an association of species and its environment between which energy and information are regularly cycled, the ecosystem in lower forms of life and in human populations exhibits significant differences and some striking parallels. The former have been minimized and the latter enlarged upon by Margelef's (1968) convincing argument for the absence of closure and for the variability of processes in biotic ecosystems. Findings of that nature are bound to foster theoretical exchanges between subdivisions of the inclusive field.

The Individual and the Ecosystem

Given the assumption that adaptation is a system phenomenon, what, it may be asked, is the position of the individual in ecological theory? Briefly stated, theoretically, the individual is a postulate; methodologically, the individual is a unit of measurement. As a postulate, five characteristics of the individual are noted.

First, as a living organism every human being requires

access to environment. That is the only source of sustenance and of knowledge needed for the procurement of sustenance. Environmental dependence is a continuous and ever-present fact of life. Its implications pervade every sphere of the human being's existence.

Second, for every individual, interdependence with other human beings is imperative. It is indispensable to life. While that is true of every living being, it is so in exceptional degree in the human being's case because of the naked state in which the individual enters the world, the long period of postnatal maturation, and the very generalized physical equipment possessed for dealing with the external world. Interdependence is the irreducible connotation of sociality. Moreover, interdependence makes possible the simultaneous conduct of two or more distinct but related activities, a feat of which the isolated individual is quite incapable. Hence the individual always occurs as a member of a population; he or she cannot live otherwise.

Third, the human individual, not unlike other organisms, is time-bound—is a finite creature in a finite world. The recurring needs for food and rest set a fundamental rhythm of life and regulate the allocation of time to all other activities. The life cycle, with its immature, mature, and senescent phases, imposes the outer limits to the time available to the individual. Given that a number of individuals must act in concert to cope with the exigencies of environments, the economization of time becomes a major preoccupation of human life.

The human being, fourth, possesses an inherent tendency to preserve and expand life to the maximum attainable under prevailing conditions (Simon 1962). That inner drive constitutes a generalized motive of which all other motives are special cases. In its most elementary manifestation, the enlargement of life is evident in the multiplication of person-years of life through either the leaving of progeny or the extension of longevity. The impulse is displayed, too, in all efforts to facilitate and secure access to environment and to multiply interdependences. If one wishes an indication of the human being's insurgent tendency, one has only to consider the spread of human settlement over every climatic zone as well as the enormous increase of numbers and the great increase of longevity that have occurred in the career of mankind.

Finally, the intrinsic limitation on the human being's behavioral variability is indeterminate. Expansiveness is unimpeded by any known restriction on the kind or the extent of refinement of activity in which the human individual can engage. When skeleton, muscles, and stamina are pressed to their utmost, the human individual's inventiveness comes into play to devise techniques for mobilizing and expending energy. This is not to say that limitations do not exist. It seems rather that externally imposed limitations become operative long before the intrinsic limits are reached.

What is not inherent in the individual's genetic equipment is the interindividual relationship—a property that emerges only in an aggregate of two or more human beings. Moreover, it is essential to the activation of all postulated characteristics. The social system, or human ecosystem, as a fabric of emergent relationships, is a phenomenon sui generis. Just as the individual is qualitatively different from the aggregate of cells composing the body, so is the social system qualitatively different from the collection of individuals in which it is observed. It follows, therefore, that the assumptions governing explanations of individual behavior are not transferable to explanations of systemic events. Instead of viewing behavior as simply neural responses to sensory stimuli, in the system context behavior is treated as activity patterned by a structure of relationships and subject to changes in that structure. Human ecology, in sum, is a macrolevel approach to the study of human organization.

None of what has been said should be construed as a denial of the human being's capacity for rationality or of a human's exercise of that capacity. On the contrary, all human behavior is assumed to be rational in the sense that it involves a calculation of means to ends. Yet purposefulness in the individual has no necessary outcome in the aggregate. The question to be asked in an ecological approach is not why persons do what they do, but under what conditions do given actions occur. That question leads one inescapably to an examination of the structural factors present in the occasion of the behavior in question. Although the study of ecosystem structure is important in its own right, it also uncovers numerous specific problems lying outside its purview which can be referred to other disciplines.

Although cultivated initially and persistently by sociologists, human ecology has had a rather grudging acceptance in the discipline of sociology by most sociologists. Textbooks on sociological theory rarely mention the subject. One might surmise that is because ecologically minded sociologists have not seen their role as one of emulating Weber, Durkheim, Simmel, Tönnies, Sorokin, or other contributors to the discipline, because they have made little or no use of motivational, attitudinal, or other psychological variables and because the theoretical import of the subject has been obscured by an early preoccupation with spatial distributions. Nor has the subject yielded to the partitioning of the facts of human collective life among the several social science fields of inquiry. The ecological mode of stating its problem as often as not contemplates the use of facts commonly thought to belong only to economics, political science, or anthropology, as well as to sociology. Human ecology is an attempt to deal holistically with the phenomenon of organization. I must say, however, that without sociological knowledge the ecological perspective cannot be adequately informed.

The Human Ecology Paradigm

The meaning of human ecology may now be stated as a paradigm composed of three propositions. They are: (1) adaptation proceeds through the formation of interdependences among the members of a population; (2) system development continues, ceteris paribus, to the maximum size and complexity afforded by the technology for transportation and communication possessed by the population; and (3) system development is resumed with the acquisition of new information that increases the capacity for the movement of materials, people, and messages and continues until the enlarged capacity is fully utilized. These may be characterized as the adaptive, the growth, and the evolution propositions, respectively.

The adaptation proposition assumes several basic elements of ecological theory. A definition of the term holds that adaptation is realized with the establishment of a viable relation between population and environment. Viability in the first instance is represented in the formation of a system. But how the effectiveness of a system is to be measured—as durability, productivity, or efficiency, or all together—is open to debate.

More difficult is the determination of when a relationship has attained whatever quality is accepted. Any decision on that score tends to be tautological. That embarrassment is avoided, however, by regarding adaptation as a process rather than as an end state. All human effort may be said to be directed toward adaptation. The issue concerns the form the adaptative efforts take.

The adaptive form is described in the second proposition as a system of relationships, that is, an organization that enables a population to act as a unit. The elemental generality of organization as an adaptive mechanism is expressed by Weiss (1971, 30) in the following:

> The primacy of the organized state of a living system thus becomes axiomatic, and there is nothing in our practical experience in cellular and developmental biology that would justify the illusion that freely operating genes can be the "source" of organization of the developing system in the sense of imposing order *de novo* on an extra-genetic matrix not already in possession of an organization of its own.

An important caveat, however, is that while a system is the only mechanism of adaptation available to human beings, as well as other living beings, it is not invariably adaptive. The system may be inappropriate, incomplete, or otherwise unsuited to a given environment. There is no necessity that any given system should survive. Further, while the view of a system as more or less continuously in process of adaptation seems to lie close to the truth, variations in rate of change may range from nearly imperceptible alterations to quantum leaps forward. This has opened the possibility for use of an equilibrium concept as an analytical tool. A system, it may be argued, tends to move toward equilibrium, and the conditions of equilibrium can be specified, as will be done in a later connection. But whether any given equilibrium state is adaptive calls for a normative judgment and, as I have said, leads one into a circular argument.

The view of a system as an adaptive mechanism draws attention to its function as a producer of sustenance. This is not to say, as does Marx (1904, 20–21) and more recently Harris (1979), that the production function underlies and determines the character of social and political institutions, as though the latter had no producing effect. It is rather that the entire system in all of its aspects is a producer of the wherewithal for life. Some parts of the system are directly involved in production, such as the manufacturing and distributing industries; other parts participate indirectly in the production of sustenance. The latter include the household, governmental, educational, health, religious, and recreational institutions. Without these the units directly engaged in production could not long continue to operate. Empirical evidence in support of this position is provided in studies demonstrating the close intertwining of social, political, and economic variables (Adelman and Morris 1965; Barnum 1976). The position to which these observations lead is commonly labeled materialism. That is as it should be. Human beings are earthy creatures. Of necessity we live close to the ground.

The onset of disequilibrium occasioned by a significant alteration in the environmental relationship, as stated in the third proposition of the paradigm, opens a possibility for evolutionary change. Should that occur, growth may then be resumed on a new basis and tends to extract the maximum potential for system development from the altered relation to environment. The process is, of course, far more complex than this simple statement lets it appear. A more extended discussion of the process is postponed for a later section.

In conclusion, it should be recognized that the paradigm lies largely in the realm of metatheory. As will be shown, the operationalization of the propositions becomes increasingly difficult where the pace of change is rapid.

2

Environment,

Population,

and Ecosystem

The principal components of ecological analysis are ecosystem, population, and environment. These constitute an interaction matrix that tends to move toward an equilibrium, a condition in which each factor is adapted to the other. Environment poses the problem of adaptation, population is the vital element, and ecosystem is the adaptive mechanism. It is a fundamental assumption of human ecology, in other words, that a human ecosystem is a population response to the necessity of maintaining a workable relation to environment. The intent of this chapter is to provide definitions for the three factors. Although this cannot be accomplished without some reference to their interactions, most of that topic will be reserved for later chapters.

Environment

Definition

The term *environment* denotes an open-ended concept. It includes all that is external to and potentially or actually influential upon an object of investigation. Accordingly it must be defined anew for each separate object. The environment of a population is different from that of an individual, and it is again different for a set of populations. Thus the object under study is of decisive importance in defining the term. As Philip Wagner (1960, 6) said: "An environment is only an environment in relation to something that it environs." The clarity of its definition, in each particular application, then, is determined by the sharpness of the boundary between internal and external, or object and not-object. Some objects may be so loosely integrated and amorphous as to have no clear limits; others are such highly coordinated systems that there is no question of their possessing unit character. Differences of this nature are commonplace among populations. A crowd on a city street is hardly comparable with the residents of a community. But since the degree of difference may be microscopic, difficult of observation, and subject to peculiarities of perspective, the identification of environment is often somewhat arbitrary.

Yet, while it may not be possible to eliminate the element of uncertainty entirely, in principle environment is distinguishable by its operation in accordance with laws different from those that govern the internal workings of an object under study (Barker 1960, 8). Environment is vastly greater in scope and in heterogeneity of content than is any individual object. Hence the impingement of environmental events on an object located at a particular time and place appears subject to a large degree of randomness. But some of the difference in governing principle, it must be admitted, is due to observer selectivity. The student asks specific questions about an object or class of objects and not all possible questions. He or she seeks answers, moreover, within a context of controlled conditions selected from among an indefinite number of conditions.

Flexible as the concept is, nevertheless it constitutes a set of conditions that command attention. It poses the basic problem of life. Environment is the source of energy and of the materials and circumstances that may be employed to extract that energy. In both of these respects environment is very unevenly constituted. In some places energy supplies are abundant and readily accessible, in others supplies are plentiful but difficult to reach, and in still other places the environment is relatively barren. Moreover, the set of external conditions is subject to temporal variations, sometimes rhythmical as with the seasons, sometimes spasmodic as in instances of upheaval, holocaust, or invasion.

Environment as Cause

The salient question has to do with the nature of environmental influence. In general, the position adopted on this issue is that environment is an independent variable, or rather a set of independent variables. The most extreme expression of this position is that of environmental determinism, most ably argued by Ratzel (1882–91) and Semple (1911). According to these authors, the physical environment is a necessary and sufficient cause not only of social systems in the broad sense but of specific intellectual, artistic, and moral artifacts as well. So exaggerated a claim was easily countered with anthropological evidence indicating the coexistence of diverse cultures in given physiographic and climatic regions (Kroeber 1939; Steward 1955). A more moderate view of the nature of environmental influence was put forward by the French geographer Vidal de la Blache (1926), which he phrased as "possibilism." Environment, according to Vidal de la Blache, is nothing more than a permissive and limiting condition, a necessary but not a sufficient cause.

There the matter rested for some thirty years. Betty Meggars then reopened the debate with a stronger than customary statement of the determining effects of environment. Her hypothesis is that the level to which a culture can develop is dependent upon the agricultural potentiality of the environment it occupies (1954, 1957). Employing South American materials, Meggars classified habitats by their agricultural potential and observed that in each class a correlated level of aboriginal technology and social organization occurred. She cited instances of failures by peoples with higher-order cultures to colonize areas with low-productivity capacities.

In a careful review of Meggars's work, Edwin Ferdon (1959) has shown that her classification of areas by agricultural potential involved a mixture of natural and cultural features. Her argument was somewhat circular therefore. Ferdon reclassified the same areas on the basis of temperature, precipitation, soil, and land form. With agricultural potential defined in these terms, the set of classes obtained proved to have no correlation with the level of cultural achievement, either pre-historically or contemporaneously. The author concluded that interactions with other groups or societies, rather than with the natural environment, controls the level to which a given organization develops.[1]

Of course, in the short run, or given minimum interference from without, any particular relationship with environment necessitates appropriate accommodations in many, if not all, sectors of a social system. Instances of that limiting effect are numerous. Webb (1931, 385ff.) has described how the settlement of pioneers in the Great Plains of America required modifications of the land laws brought with them from the East. Laws regulating the size of farm holdings were relaxed to permit the very extensive use of land required in a semiarid zone. Similarly, English common law pertaining to water rights was found inapplicable in a vast area of water scarcity. Instead of water rights being confined to riparian lands, they were extended to all beneficial uses, for example, irrigation, on nonriparian lands. An instance of a somewhat different kind concerned industrial development in four regions situated on different segments of the Austrasian coal field extending from Belgium through northern France and into the Ruhr Valley (Wrigley 1961). Although technology, capital, and labor were comparable in each region, during the period 1850 to 1914 industrial growth advanced much further where the coal seams were near the surface and easy to mine. Growth was slow where the seams were deep and convoluted.

Classificatory Principles

Thinking of environment solely in physical and biotic terms is, as Ferdon has shown, manifestly a mistake. That might be a useful conception when all other things can be assumed constant, but all other things are not, in fact, constant and they too form part of the external or environing world. The variety of environmental content is enormous and subject to radical shifts from time to time. To make manageable so inclusive a concept without seriously impairing its value requires the use of a rather simple classification of components. There are at least two bases on which a classification may be built, one a measure of scope and the other a measure of duration.

The scope basis pertains to events and circumstances that

have a location relative to a habitat. For present purposes it is enough to recognize a distinction between the biophysical class and the ecumenic class of environmental elements. The former includes physiographic features, climate, soil characteristics, plant and animal life, mineral and other materials, and the altered forms of those elements resulting from man's occupance and use of an area. The ecumenic environment comprises the ecosystems or cultures possessed by peoples in adjacent areas and beyond; it comprises the universe to which access is provided by the existing facilities for transportation and communication. I use the term *ecumenic* not out of preference for baroque language but to avoid the accumulation of meaning in terms such as *social* or *economic*. Perhaps it should be noted that the relative importance of each of these two large categories of external conditions varies in different times and places. In any given situation the one set of conditions may appear to have such immediacy and such overwhelming importance that the other is made to seem insignificant.

Group isolation, as assumed implicitly by Meggars, is at most a relative condition. Lesser has pointed out that every residence group, band, or village lives in a "social field" composed of a number of other residence groups among which exchange relations are maintained (1961, 40–48). Viewed in a different way, this phenomenon is seen as a set of juxtaposed micro-environments. Each group obtains from its particular habitat not only most of the raw materials used in its daily life, but also one or more materials useful to other groups in its vicinity. Those surplus or unique materials provide a basis on which the given group develops exchange relationships in a "social field." Therein lies the beginning of an intergroup division of labor. Archaeologists have observed that localities where a number of differentiated habitats occurred in close proximity were particularly favorable for cultural interchanges and the advance of organization (Braidwood and Willey 1962, 354–55). A number of habitats have been identified in the Euphrates Valley (Adams 1965, 48). In Mesoamerica, where the Aztec civilization flourished, one may encounter, over a distance of sixty to eighty kilometers, "nearly all of the world's environments" (Sanders and Price 1968, 101).

Although biophysical and ecumenic elements of environment are readily distinguishable, they impinge upon one another in various ways. Relations with the one class of elements are usually sustained at least in part with the aid of relations with the other class of elements. This is nicely illustrated by the circumstances underlying the depopulation of the inland areas of northern Alaska. The Eskimos of that region, whose economy was based largely on the caribou, relied on trade relations with the coastal Eskimos for blubber, oil, and other supplementary materials, in return for which they exchanged caribou skins. But when the coastal Eskimos established trade relations with Europeans, from whom they obtained more attractive items, they abandoned their trade with the inland Eskimos. In consequence, the latter could no longer continue their traditional mode of life in the inland region; they left the area for resettlement in the coastal region (Spencer 1959, 28, 172, 204). A modern example, of which there are many instances, is found in deserted mining areas. The Michigan copper mines, as a case in point, tap the world's richest lodes. Yet as their shafts grew deeper and the costs of operation mounted, a cheap electrolytic refining process was developed that enabled deposits of low-grade ores, though located far from consumption centers, to capture the copper market. Michigan mines thereupon were shut down and the population of their region left stranded (Goodrich, Allin, and Thornwaite 1936, chap. 8).

The second or duration basis that must be acknowledged in a classification of environmental conditions has to do with their regularity of occurrence. Within both the biophysical and the ecumenic classes may be distinguished constant and variable conditions. The former comprise the more or less permanent characteristics of an area, such as elevation, drainage, soil type, the flora and fauna, rhythmic oscillations, represented in diurnal and seasonal cycles, and the presence of other human settlements. The variable conditions include the irregularly occurring or unpredictable events that impinge upon an area, such as volcanic eruptions, storms, the swarming of insect and animal populations, visitations from other human groups, hostile invasions, and cultural diffusion. The exhibit on the following page arrays the territorial and the temporal classes relative to one another.

The constant conditions define the initial adaptive problem confronting a population that takes up residence in an area. Adaptation is a process of interaction. On the one hand, occupance of an area works changes in the constant conditions by

ENVIRONMENT CLASSIFICATION

SCOPE	DURATION	
	Constant	*Variable*
Biophysical	Land forms, flora and fauna, rhythmic oscillations	Eruptions, storms, swarming of populations
Ecumenic	Human groups in accessible areas, exchange relations	Visits of strangers, migrations, information flows

affecting soil content, altering the species composition of plant and animal life, or by modifying the terrain with buildings, pathways, dams, and the like. On the other hand, the changed conditions react upon the residence group to require modifications of behavior and to set different limits on the amount of time and energy needed to maintain a given level of living. As the interaction continues over time, the swings from action to reaction narrow and a stable environmental relationship tends to be established.

Variations in the conditions comprising the environment of an organized population may be of different orders of magnitude. They may be so weak as to no more than produce a short-term deviation from an existing pattern. Or they may so alter or rearrange the constant conditions that a new adaptation must be undertaken. It is probable that all ecosystem change is initiated by environmental variation. Of this much more will be said in a later chapter.

The consequences of variations in the ecumenic environment can be quite different from those that occur in the biophysical environment. If variations occur only in the latter class of conditions, their effects cannot be cumulative. A population will be forced to alter its way of life to take into account the shifts in or disappearances from its biophysical habitat, and in doing so it will tend to drop from its repertory forms of behavior that are no longer appropriate. Or, in response to a temporal variation, a group tends simply to suspend a given activity until a normal state is restored. In neither instance will anything have been added to its capacity to accumulate knowledge or techniques. The group may or may not survive the change. By contrast, disturbances that emanate from the ecumenic environment are in their nature susceptible to an accumulation. Variability in the ecumenic environment is unique in another respect. The ecumenic environment as well as the group environed is subject to cumulative change. Largely for this reason, the limits of the cumulative potential in an ecosystem are indeterminate. It is for the same reason, furthermore, that the ratio of constant to variable elements tends to be lower in the ecumenic than in the biophysical environment.

Given the inclusive composition of environment, its operationalization for research purposes poses a problem. The difficulty must be circumvented rather than resolved. This is accomplished by turning to an indicator that captures potentiality instead of actuality. Such an indicator exists in the form of access as measured by extent and number of avenues of contact with externalities. Where the values of those measures are minimal, an environment is local and composed primarily of biophysical elements. As access is increased, the ecumenic environment is enlarged and the composition becomes more heterogeneous.

These comments call attention to certain properties commonly attributed to environment, namely, space and time. As I have said before, environmental elements are very unevenly distributed; indeed were that not true, it is unlikely the idea of distance would have occurred to the human being. The distances among selected environmental features mark off spaces with differing compositions. But neither distance nor space is an absolute. Each is experienced as the time required to move from point to point. And that, as I shall later show, is contingent on how a population is organized. In other words, space and time are dimensions employed by man for the measurement of his environment.

The implications of the complex character of the environmental relationship should be drawn with care. It is unwise, for example, to conclude that, since a population always confronts its environment in terms of the ecosystem it possesses, the population creates its environment in the image of that system. Many have yielded to this temptation, apparently

unaware of the logically precarious position into which they
have been led. In collapsing two variables—environment and
ecosystem—into one, they deprive themselves of a principal
source of causation. Thereafter all human events are self-
generative. To avoid that cultural solipsism it is imperative
that environment be preserved as a distinct and separate class
of phenomena.

Population

Definition

From a denotative standpoint the population concept is quite
simple. A population is defined as any quantity of things that
conform to a given definition (Boulding 1934). The term is thus
applicable to a great variety of collections of things, and it is
often so used. Virtually every phenomenon can be conceived
in aggregate, that is, population, terms. A beach is an aggregate of grains of sand, a language is an aggregate of words, a
living body is an aggregate of cells, and a society is an aggregate of persons. An emphasis upon a common characteristic
shared by all units of a phenomenon obviously obscures many
differences. Nevertheless the aggregate view has considerable
utility, at least for various preliminary purposes. The number
of persons who comprise a society gives a rough indication of
the society's capacity for collective action. In the same vein,
size comparisons of different societies are useful for what they
imply relative to differences in the capabilities. Changes in
size, moreover, are unquestionable indicators of important
changes in the structure of a society, though the natures of the
changes are not indicated thereby.

A conception of population as merely an aggregate of discrete units may serve some purposes adequately enough, but
it is misleading when applied to the components of a systemic
phenomenon. Such a view confuses a methodological tactic
with the phenomenon under observation. This is a common
tendency among statisticians, psychologists, and others with
an individualistic predilection. They are inclined to regard
complex events as composed of units that are additive rather
than multiplicative. The aggregate is the reductionist's view of
social reality. To describe an ecosystem in terms of the number

of people composing it does not belie its integrity as an entity. Population is one of several dimensions of an ecosystem; others include the space occupied, the number of functional positions, the number of combinations of functional positions, the energy generated, and so forth. The meanings of these enumerations are not, of course, implicit in their quantities. Thus a birth rate is not just an aggregate of births divided by an aggregate of potential reproducers. It is a measure of the way in which an ecosystem is meeting its replacement needs. Similarly a migration rate is a response of the society to a redistribution of its opportunities. The aggregate with which ecology deals, it will be recalled, is a population of environmentally oriented, necessarily dependent, time-bound, compulsively expansive, and extraordinarily adaptive individuals.

Properties of the Aggregate

If I may stay for a moment with the conception of population as an aggregate, it may be shown to possess a number of properties that are not shared by the individuals composing it. For one thing, a population is composed of parts that are capable of independent mobility. Consequently a population has no special temporal or spatial form. Its members can be arranged in an indefinite number of combinations and patterns. Obviously that is not true of the individual organism, for its parts are so specialized that they cannot operate other than in specific relationships with other parts. Further, the parts of a population, human beings, are interchangeable or replaceable. Any individual not in a population can be substituted for one that is so long as the former possesses the characteristics by which the population is defined. Nor is this the case with the parts of individual organisms. Their specialization eliminates the possibility of interchangeability and makes replaceability extremely difficult.

Unlike the individual organism again, a population has no intrinsic limit to its longevity. Since it is not itself an organism, a population has no organic processes and hence no life cycle. A population is also without any limitations on its size. It may range from as few as two to an indefinitely large number of members. While the size of an organism is determined in large part by its genetic constitution, the size of a population is influenced primarily by external circumstances.

A Demographic System

Aggregate properties such as those described underlie a simple demographic system. That is to say, under certain conditions, demographic attributes and processes interact systematically to create a predictable structure. The attributes in question are age and sex, and the processes are birth and death rates. The processes may also be regarded as biological mechanisms through which environmental influences operate upon an aggregate.

Given any particular mix of age and sex characteristics subject to a particular and unchanging set of birth and death rates, within a knowable period of time the processes will produce a symmetrical distribution of the attributes. With reference to age, this distribution involves a series of cohorts diminishing in size from youngest to oldest that, when diagrammed in a bar graph, appears as an isosceles triangle (Ryder 1961). The perpendicular of the triangle divides the age distribution into nearly equal sex categories. The lack of exact equality is traceable to genetic factors that cause males to be born in somewhat larger numbers than females (105 to 100) and result in males dying at slightly higher rates than females.

A change in birth or death rates alters the age composition. Thus, if death rates decline while birth rates remain unchanged, all cohorts increase in size, but the major part of the increase occurs at the infant level. A larger-than-normal youthful cohort enters the population and creates distortions in the symmetry of the structure as it moves along the life span. If the birth-death relationship persists, the average age of the population declines. Or, on the other hand, if birth rates decline while death rates remain unchanged, a smaller-than-normal infant cohort enters the population, and as it grows older the sizes of age categories successively decline. The cumulative effect is to raise the average age. There are, of course, various other combinations of changes in birth and death rates, and each one produces knowable effects on the demographic structure. It should also be recognized that changes in age composition react upon birth and death rates to affect their magnitude: since rates are weighted averages, changes in the weights, that is, numbers in age and sex categories, alter the averages.

In short, a population tends to have a set of processes by

which it responds to environmental shifts and from which it derives a given structure. The qualifying condition alluded to earlier has to do with the extent to which a population possesses unit character.

Population as a Unit

In most usages of the term, the reference is to specific populations rather than to population in general. Hence the possession by the members of a common intrinsic characteristic is not enough; there must also be a differentially held extrinsic characteristic that distinguishes clusters of numbers from one another. That, as practice amply shows, turns out to be a temporal-spatial boundary of some kind. The term *population* is applied to the residents of a continent, a region, or a smaller territorial subdivision. Each step in the narrowing of the boundary tends to be a closer approximation, other things constant, to an aggregate whose members are capable of acting in concert, of engaging in an organized response to environment. They might do that, for example, by virtue of sharing a common technical culture and a homogeneous territory. The uniform conduct of a subsistence household economy by each of many peasant families scattered over an area represents a unit response of a sort. But it is a statistical rather than a systemic unity. Actually the occupants of the area should be regarded not as a single population but as a number of separate household populations. The several households are not united by any organizing principle. A capability for a unitary response to environment requires that an aggregate have acquired an inclusive organization. Only then will it possess a single system of internal processes that can distribute the effects of environmental influences throughout the whole. A population, then, is an aggregate with unit character, and unit character having any operational significance is contingent on the presence of organization. Population and organization enter into the definitions of one another; population is bounded by the territorial extent of organization, and organization is visible only in a population (Hawley 1969).

It is worth noting that the aggregate properties mentioned earlier contribute to the attainment and persistence of organization in a population and of a unitary response to environment. The independent mobility of parts, for example, is essential to the formation of an organization where none ex-

isted previously. That attribute permits functional differentiation, the grouping of differentiated parts in various kinds of
operating clusters, and an appropriate distribution in time and
space of the clustered specialists. Independent mobility also
makes possible a reshuffling of parts and a reconstitution of
functional clusters as forces of change play upon an aggregate.
Interchangeability of parts or members, even though narrowed to certain specifications by functional differentiation,
lends stability to each functional cluster and to an entire system of clusters. Threats of disruptions arising from death or
the deterioration of members can be contained and turned
aside, for new parts can be substituted for old.

The absence of any constitutional restriction on the size of a
population provides yet another source of resilience. The
aggregate can be expanded or contracted in response to changing environmental conditions; its adaptive capacity is unin-
hibited by a fixed size. The formation of a system of relationships, of course, involves some loss of resilience, just as
specialization proceeds at the cost of versatility. Nevertheless,
there is a measure of flexibility in a population that could not
otherwise be present. Unlimited longevity reinforces the interchangeability of parts in contributing durability to a population. The continuity realizable thereby fosters the development and accumulation of permanent products. While this
bears most importantly on the system of relationships that
might be developed, it applies also to the instrumentalities of a
system, such as tools, buildings, and other acquisitions.

Equilibrium Population

Equilibrium as applied to population is apt to be most readily
visible as stability of size through time. Upon analysis, however, constant size is found to involve two parameters—one
demographic, the other organizational.

A demographic equilibrium is indicated when births are
just sufficient to replace deaths and the age composition corresponds to what is expected from a long-term balance of
births and deaths, that is, the age composition of an appropriate life table. Those characteristics have the greatest probability of occurrence in an isolated situation, for otherwise they
would be subject to distortions arising from a high incidence of
environmental variations. Since isolation is most nearly

approximated in populations that have minimal control of their biophysical environment, they normally have high death rates—on the order of thirty-five to forty per one thousand members of the population—and comparable birth rates. Thus an expected age composition in such a population has about 30 percent under fifteen years of age, 60 percent between ages fifteen and sixty years, and 10 percent over sixty years of age.

But a demographic equilibrium is doubtless more often an average than a permanent state. Disturbances of one kind or another invariably occur, and if the magnitudes are great enough to alter the death or the birth rates, they leave their effects on the age and sometimes the sex compositions. The distribution by sex, unlike that for age, has an intrinsic stability owing to its initial determination by chromosomal combinations at the time of cell fertilization. Yet it is sensitive to mortality fluctuations. Environmentally induced mortality risks usually impinge most severely upon males, while institutionally created risks, notably infanticide, tend to be selective of females. The main effects of disturbance in the life situation, however, are manifested in the age distribution. Thus even after vital rates return to a replacement level—that is, birth and death rates are equal—after a disturbance, the absolute numbers of births and deaths are rendered unequal by virtue of the distortions introduced into the age composition. Quite often, as noted earlier, this results in a growth momentum that must spend itself before a demographic equilibrium can be restored.

A demographic equilibrium, of course, cannot be an independent event. It can only occur under conditions of a given environmental relationship. The classic formulation of the population-environment relationship is that proposed by Thomas Malthus (1798). According to Malthus, because population is able to increase geometrically while resources can only be increased arithmetically, population invariably tends to outrun the food supply. As numbers accumulate relative to available resources, the excess of births over deaths declines to zero, largely due to a rise in the death rate. Growth ceases at a size that can be maintained at no better than a bare subsistence level. This was demonstrated experimentally in a fruit fly population by Raymond Pearl (1930).

Although Malthus later modified the conclusion, derived from the logical extension of his initial assumptions, by the addition of "moral restraint," that is, delayed marriage together with sexual continence, as a check on growth, he did not develop the full implications of the new element in his argument. He failed to give sufficient weight to the controlling influence of the ecosystem, for which age at marriage is but a partial index. That was left to his critics. Anthropologists, for example, have observed in their field studies that population densities in simple groups are usually well below what the biophysical environment can support (Binford 1968; Lee 1979; Wilkinson 1973). It has also been pointed out many times over that a given habitat is capable of supporting varying densities of population, depending on the type of ecosystem possessed by the occupants.

Population as Cause

There is a general predilection for inferring from Malthusian theory that population change is a primary cause of technological and organizational change. This had one of its more recent expressions in Mark Cohen's (1977) contention that the beginning of settled agriculture was due to population increase. He cites evidence that shows that nomadic peoples in different parts of the world knew about food seeds, their selection, and domestication. But, according to Cohen, they had no reason to put the knowledge into practice until population growth created a food crisis in each of many occupied areas. Cohen's argument takes population increase as a given. Causation is not so simple a matter, however.

A postulate stated in the preceding chapter specifies an expansiveness inherent in all forms of life, mankind included. In a population, that expansiveness is compounded, constituting a dynamic potential of considerable power. The expansive propensity does not need to be regarded as uniformly held among the members of a population. Genetic and experiential differences will create diversity on that score. What is assumed, however, is that in populations comparable in size and incidence of cross-breeding with other populations, the range of differences in the expansive propensity tends to be approximately equal. In large populations the stability in range of differences is presumably greater than in small populations. Thus any sizeable population may be expected to include enough members with expansive propensities strong or suitable enough to enable them to accept and cultivate new opportunities.

Accordingly population tends to fill all available resource space. In a rather limited sense, then, population is capable of acting as an efficient cause. The expansive power, however, is held in check by the personnel requirements of the system in which it is organized. Stated differently, resource space is defined by the technology and organization of the system. Any change in the system that increases resource space is followed by a decline in the death rate and a surge of population growth. As the added number needed to utilize the increased resource space is approached, the birth rate enters upon a decline, seeking the level of the death rate, and growth subsides.

But expansiveness is not manifested only in the addition of number. A population seizes upon any opportunity to enlarge its resource space, even after its ratio of numbers to system requirements has approached equilibrium. That is expressed in the accumulation of capital goods and increases in income per capita. Increments in those respects feed back to population as extensions of longevity. Added years of life may either supplement or substitute for increases of number. Longevity increase is no less a manifestation of expansiveness than is an excess of births over deaths.

Without population there can be no adaptive organization. People of various kinds and in various numbers are necessary to carry on the several activities through which they normally support one another. This point is cogently argued by Boserup (1976). It does not follow, of course, that the mere presence of an assemblage of people assures the appearance of a system of any particular kind or, for that matter, of any system at all. A crowd on a city street, the audience in the theater, or the occupants of a large land mass are aggregates without systems. And lacking organization they are unable to give expression to an expansive propensity. In other words, although population possesses some properties of an efficient cause, it can only operate as such under certain conditions. In the absence of those conditions, its effect is that of a necessary condition. Without population a system cannot occur, but in the presence of population a system does not invariably occur.

It is in the nature of a necessary condition that its modification or elimination alters a fundamental support for an existing organization. An organization cannot continue to operate in the usual way when there are no longer enough people to staff its positions. Exceptional losses of population, such as that brought about by the Black Death in the fourteenth century (Buer 1926; Gottfried 1983) or by large-scale emigrations from relatively small areas,[2] require drastic institutional accommodations. They must be scaled down to simpler divisions of labor and to lesser clienteles.

On the other hand, excess population occurs occasionally. It results from discontinuities in change. A seasonal decline in animal predators or crop pests will allow an increase in food supply and a consequent decline in mortality. A limited increase in the productivity of an organization will have a similar effect. But once begun, population change carries beyond short-term alterations in life conditions, for larger-than-normal birth cohorts have been added to the population. If system change does not continue in ways that enable it to utilize the excess number, the excess is dumped into out-migration streams or into a rising mortality.

The expansive power of population notwithstanding, it cannot operate independent of organizational circumstances. In and of itself it cannot cause war, resource exhaustion, or environmental pollution, as Malthusians have argued. Such outcomes are explained as due to maladaptations or malfunctioning of organization.

The Ecosystem

Definition

Briefly stated, an ecosystem is an arrangement of mutual dependences in a population by which the whole operates as a unit and thereby maintains a viable environmental relationship.[3] Population and system, I have said, are different aspects of the same thing; one is the quantitative aspect of which the other is the substantive aspect. The use of the word *arrangement* in the definition asserts the presence of a more or less stable ordering of parts, a structure that endures through time. Among other things, structure implies the existence of properties that cannot be distributed to the parts. But structure, far from being a rigid framework of beams and trusses, is in this usage composed of a set of active parts that engage in routinized movements. Rhythmic actions and interactions hold the parts in constant relation to one another and thereby preserve form and identity. Structure, it has been said, is function at rest, while function is structure in motion (Dewey 1925, 71–72).

Unit character implies the existence of a boundary, an outer limit that marks off an entity in a field of observation and makes it recognizable. The operationalization of the boundary concept, however, often comes down to a matter of definition. Ecosystems perversely tend to be frayed at their edges, especially where they encroach upon one another. An indicator of boundary location, however, is contained in the definition of a social system. Since a system embraces all interactions that recur with a prescribed periodicity, the boundary falls where that periodicity no longer obtains. The periodicity may be hourly, daily, weekly, or seasonally. "Systemness" may then be thought of as tapering off on an interaction frequency gradient. The angle of the gradient's slope varies with the complexity of the system.

While the system concept is adopted in this volume as a useful way of regarding the ecological entity, it is not without its critics. It has been questioned, for example, by Kenneth Wilkinson in a provocative essay entitled "The Community as a Social Field" (1970). As the title suggests, the author prefers the notion of "field" conceived as a fluid matrix of interacting forces in which emergent properties are more distinctive than are structural properties. The proposal is intriguing. But upon analysis its merit hangs upon what the author elects to study and what he wants to explain. Evidently Wilkinson wishes to give greater emphasis to the dynamic than to the structural aspects of organized life. That the field is "boundless," or that it is without structural continuities, as Wilkinson implies, is doubtful. A field of forces such as a community is certainly dense at the center and thins out with distance away from the center. Although not absolute, there is a boundary. Again, if there are no continuities of structure, how can the field be recognized in successive observations? The concept, in short, offers no escape from some of the elementary problems of system theory. The notion of an interaction field is indispensable, however; the problem is how to reconcile the field and systems concepts.

An ecosystem does not spring into being instantaneously. It has a history, conceivably a natural history, in the course of which it has moved from murky beginnings through a simple to a more complex form. But the origins are rarely, if ever, accessible to observation, though reconstructions of prehistory provide refracted glimpses into beginnings. Thus, the student must begin the analysis with an ecosystem in relatively mature form. For the sake of convenience we may start with the notion of system in the most general terms. That will portray a system in its rudiments and as an entity in a stable state. First there are some additional concepts in need of clarification.

Technology, Culture, and the Ecosystem

Technology is a term used to denote the practical arts and is commonly construed to include only tools and the methods for their use. Such a narrow definition, however, cannot stand close inspection. For just as tools are inseparable from methods, so are methods lodged in cooperative arrangements of various kinds. Thus the use of the horse is usually embedded in a military, an agricultural, or a transportation institution, and in most cases it requires the collaboration of the leather workers for harness, the metallurgist for shoes, and the farmer for food. There are instances in which tools and methods cannot be distinguished. Science, for example, a tool for the discovery of knowledge, consists of a set of methods practiced in a collegium of investigators. Likewise many customs are methods for accomplishing objectives of vital importance. Incest taboos assure an extension of kinship and of mutual aid obligations, formal marriage is a technique for establishing the inheritance rights of children, and the corporation serves the purpose of assembling capital while limiting liability. Technology, in short, is the instrumental aspect of culture (Cole 1968, 61–62; Boulding 1969, 126–40; Arrow 1971, 224; Brooks 1980, 139; Kuznets 1978, 335).

Technology and *culture* are both classificatory terms for elements, that is, behavior patterns, of an ecosystem. It is quite appropriate to resolve a whole into its parts for purposes of analysis. So techniques and all other routinized behaviors may be separated for sorting, counting, and intensive examination. Furthermore, insofar as they can be transported individually from one place to another, they may seem to have a unitary and additive character. But the meaning of the communicated or diffused behavior pattern is restored only after it has been integrated into the structure of a receiving system, and then, of course, the meaning may be different from what it possessed in its donor system. Some behavior patterns are more transportable than are others. The use of a gun is fairly easy to communicate. Much more difficult to transmit are the techniques for its manufacture and maintenance. Still more resistant to communication from one system to another is an ethical principle. But the transportability of a behavior pattern should not be mistaken for independence of meaning. Meaning is totally dependent on the organization of relationships and activities in which a given behavior is practiced.

Culture, and its subclass technology, and organization or system are different facets of the same phenomenon. Culture is ecosystem viewed analytically; ecosystem is culture viewed synthetically.

System Elements: Units, Relations, Functions

A system is analyzable into certain unique properties. These may be reduced to their elements as units, relations, and functions. They are combined in various ways, as we shall later see, to constitute more elaborate properties. Here a caveat is necessary. System properties are not to be confused with "system prerequisites" as used by functional theorists (Malinowski 1938; Parsons 1951; Levy 1952). The idea expressed in the latter phrase is not only redundant, it prejudges what is actually a problematic matter. In the present state of knowledge and of theoretical development it seems advisable to phrase an argument in a way that permits an easy translation of its derivations into probabilistic terms.

Units. The units of a social system are those entities that enter into relationships with one another on the basis of the functions they perform. They appear in simple and complex forms. Simple units are individuals; complex units are combinations of individuals of various kinds. The members of each class are

capable of sustaining relationships and of performing distinguishable functions, hence the term *unit*. Inasmuch as the
types of complex units are discussed at length in later sections,
I need not linger over them here.

Relations. Interdependence among the members of an aggregate occur with reference to the ways in which they can be
useful to one another. These can be reduced to two in number.
One arises from the fact that daily life requires the simultaneous conduct of a number of diverse activities, such as
obtaining food and raw materials, processing the materials,
making implements, providing child care, creating government, and so forth. Indeed, one of the chief virtues of collective living is that it permits the coincident performance of
various tasks. These are parceled out among units according to
the skills or other qualifications they possess. In consequence,
individuals complement one another in the performance of
their respective assignments; they enter into mutual dependences based on their functional differences. The term *symbiosis* is used to describe that kind of relationship. Symbiosis is
present wherever there is mutual support, for example, between complementary differences. In one of its aspects, then,
an ecosystem is a symbiotic union.

A second form of mutual dependence derives from the
existence in a population of common interests or similar tasks
that can be pursued more effectively when two or more like-
acting units pool their energies. The lifting of a heavy log, the
stroking of a large canoe, or the reaping of a harvest before a
change of weather usually require a number of individuals
acting in unison. In such instances individuals enter into
working relationships on the basis of their similarities, that is,
their ability to engage in coactions. The term for this type of
interdependence is *commensalism*, which literally means "eat-
ing from the same table." Commensalism, however, is not
confined to labor. It is applicable wherever a common interest
is at issue—in defense of a territory, in allegiance to a ruler or a
divinity, in the cultivation of an avocation, and in various
other respects. In another of its aspects, then, an ecosystem is
a set of commensalistic relationships.

It is important to note that symbiosis and commensalism are
primarily types of relationships,[4] though they serve as the
bases of distinctive complex units, as will be shown in chapter

4. The members of a population shift from one to the other, sorting themselves into different combinations, in the course of their daily and weekly rounds of activities. At one moment an individual is a specialist performing a role in the division of labor, at another time a kinsman celebrating a family ritual, and at still another moment a communicant in a religious congregation. The mutual dependences that constitute an ecosystem are a complex interweaving of symbiotic and commensalistic linkages.

It is fruitless to debate which of the two sectors is the most basic or the most important. From a superficial view the symbiotic sector appears to have a prior claim to importance. It mediates the relation of the population to its environment from which the vital flow of sustenance materials is obtained. Furthermore, the amount and kinds of sustenance materials made available fixes the degrees of freedom within which the aggregate may elaborate upon its structure. Yet these effects do not happen without support from the commensalistic sector. The effective performance of certain functions frequently hangs upon mutual supplementation among like units. Commensal unions are also important mechanisms of control and stability within the system. No doubt there may be a certain amount of inconsequentiality in the commensal sector; but not everything in the division of labor is essential either. More to the point, however, symbiotic and commensalistic sectors are analytical constructs abstracted from a single entity. To treat them in any other way is to mistake an abstraction for the reality.

Functions. Now let me return to the question of what is interrelated. It has been said that the unit, the relatum, is a member of a population. Yet even a cursory review of the history of an ecosystem—a community or a society—reveals that the personnel are among its most transitory features. Individuals come and go and generations succeed one another with measured periodicity, but the system lives on. Does that suggest there is a structure of niches or roles having an existence independent of persons? Obviously not. A structure does exist, however, independent of specific people. Any adult male can occupy the role of father; whether he performs the task well or ill is beside the point. Likewise any suitably trained person can be a hunter, a plumber, or a corporation president.

So there is something to be gained from conceiving a social system abstractly, that is, as a phenomenon apart from its actors.

If that is done, the mutual dependences comprising a system are seen to be linkages among recurring activities. The latter have been described as niches or positions when their locations in a system of relationships are the point of emphasis,[5] and as roles or functions when their operating properties are the focus of interest. Here the term *function* is used to include both static and dynamic features; a function is any repetitive activity that is reciprocated by another or other repetitive activities. The observational problem of how to identify a function is only partly resolved by this definition. There is still the question of how specific or how unmingled with other activities must a given activity be in order to qualify as a function. Is the farmer who performs a hundred different tasks in the course of his agricultural pursuit performing one or one hundred functions? Each of the many things he does is so mixed with others that any attempt to catalog them proves to be more than a little arbitrary. The wiser course is to recognize that under certain circumstances farming is a cluster of tasks constituting a single function vis-à-vis another cluster of tasks such as household maintenance performed by his wife. There are occasions, of course, in which some one of the hundred-odd tasks involved in agriculture are performed by one or a few farmers for all other farmers—storage or marketing, for example. In that event tasks become observable as separate and distinct classes of activity. This separation of tasks among acting units is referred to by the familiar term *specialization*. Specialization suggests an initial bundle of activity from which specific tasks can be peeled off successively and more or less indefinitely. We might suppose, for purposes of illustration, that every instance of collective life is sustained by a mix of activities that produce sustenance and related materials, distribute the products among the participants, maintain the number of units required to produce and distribute the products, and exercise the controls needed to assure an uninterrupted performance of all tasks with a minimum of friction. These several tasks might be merged in a continuous flow of activity that admits of no distinctions. Or they might be split apart and assigned to four different categories of actors. Again they might be minutely subdivided and spread among a large number of full-time specialists. Each advance along that path leads to the emergence of distinguishable functions. In short, functions are identifiable as such where activities have been subdivided and allocated to separate units.

So it would seem that we are brought back to the members of the population as acting units. But not necessarily so. The units to which functions are allocated are not individuals exclusively. In some instances they are clusters of individuals arranged in various combinations. The farm household is such a unit, so is the factory, the retail establishment, the government bureau. To be sure, several questions here beg for an answer. I shall return to them in a later section. At the moment it is enough to recognize that an ecosystem is an arrangement of mutual dependences among functional units, without specifying the characteristics of the units.

System Structure: The Symbiotic Sector

The symbiotic sector of a system is built about the procurement of sustenance, which is to say that it is reared upon the environmental relationship. According to the first postulate stated, every member of a population must have access to environment, for no alternative source of food and other requisite materials exists. It was also pointed out that so unspecialized is the organic equipment of the human being that survival requires the simultaneous performance of a variety of activities. Some degree of differentiation is imperative in even the simplest life situation. And it is among such differentiated activities that symbiotic relations are formed. Accordingly, the kinds of environmental access needed may differ over a wide range of possibilities, reflecting the kinds of activities in which units are routinely engaged. Differentiation of activity is associated with a differentiation of environmental requirements. Some activities are diversified in respect to soil conditions, climate, raw materials, or other external circumstances utilized. Differences occur also in the degree of directness of environmental access required. Some functions must have direct access, while others are contingent on those needing direct access and, therefore, require no more than indirect access. Contingencies of that nature may be extended to two, three, or more steps of removal from the function directly involved with environment. The processor of raw material cannot operate until the producers have provided some materials with which to work. Processors therefore must have access to producers, but not to environment directly. The distributors or traders can do nothing until some processed materials are made available for exchange. Thus traders achieve environmental access through two intervening functionaries linked in a transitive sequence. Such a sequence may be extended through several additional linked functions, each one more step removed from direct environmental access. Furthermore, the greater the differentiation of function, the greater is the proportion of all functions that are indirectly related to environment, that is, through the agency of one or more mediating functions.

The function that is directly engaged with environment is the key function. It occupies a strategic position relative to other functions. Since the key function transmits environmental inputs—materials and information—to other contingent functions, it regulates and to a considerable extent determines the conditions under which the contingent functions are performed. The controlling influence of the key function is, in the first instance, entirely inadvertent, though its strategic position may and often does provide the basis for a purposeful exercise of control. The materials and information the unit in the key function transmits to its related functions fixes the ranges of activities and interests with which other units of a system may occupy themselves. The key function also exercises regulatory influences on contingent functions through the amount of product it makes available, the rhythms with which it operates, the locations at which it is carried on, and in still other ways that derive from the idiosyncracies of the particular activity. Of these several kinds of influences, productivity is by far the most important. All other functions subsist upon the inputs generated by the key function. Stated more formally, the greater the volume of the product of the key function, the greater is the possible number of contingent functions (i.e., the extent of specialization) and the longer may be the transitive sequences in which contingent functions may be arrayed.

The key function is an essential element in the concept of an ecological system. To the extent that it is not clearly distinguishable from other activities, the system at best is tenuous and somewhat incoherent. In the extreme case in which every unit has the same relation to environment, that is, is completely self-sufficient, no system exists. Close approximations to that circumstance are found in hunting and gathering peoples, such as the Utes of the American Southwest (Steward 1933) and the !Kung of the Kalahari Desert in Africa (Lee 1979).[6] These people live in commensalistic bands composed of unstable numbers of family units. There are degrees of systemness, ranging from the loose and inchoate to the explicitly structured network of relationships. A system comes into being and gains clarity as functions are differentiated and are ordered with reference to one or a very small number of key functions.

It would be a mistake in this connection to think exclusively in terms of the biophysical environment. The key function is not always occupied with raw-material production. How it is defined is determined by the kind of environmental input that is of most critical importance to the system. Where, for example, a product of local resources is systematically traded for the products of other systems, the key function is determined by the comparative importance of production and of trade as sources of sustenance. Occasionally no distinction can be made because the producer is also the trader, two tasks combined in one functionary. Yet even before the two tasks appear as separate specialities, the requisites of trade may begin to regulate the use of local resources. Where the reliance on trade determines the use of local resources, the ecumenic environment has displaced the biophysical environment as the critical set of influences. In that event the trader occupies the key role; his function has become instrumental in relating the system to the more salient feature of environment. This points to a resolution of what otherwise appears to be an anomaly. That is, although agriculturalists may be most directly engaged in the primary production of sustenance materials, they may nevertheless occupy a subordinate position in a system. If so, it is because the value of their product has become contingent on the transportation and marketing of the product as carried on by other functionaries. In that event the mediators of the ecumenic environment have acquired precedence over the mediators of the biophysical environment.

Functional differentiation, however, exhibits more than one dimension. In addition to the positional dimension just mentioned, there is a qualitative dimension composed of two elements. One is substantive as represented in the particular type of activity involved, for example, agriculture, manufacturing, marketing, and so forth, or any of their many subdivisions. The other is the degree of skill and amount and type of information required for the conduct of each activity. To some extent these dimensions lie parallel. Type of activity specifies skill and information requirements and determines position in a relational sequence. Of no small importance is the effect the dimensions have on the reproducibility of functionally qualified units, that is, on the costs to the system of preparing a unit for a functional position. But whether costs of reproducing qualified functionaries will return corresponding benefits depends on the size of population. For every specialized activity presupposes a minimum number of users of the product of the function, a number sufficient to support the continuous conduct of the activity. Thus it may be said that the number of units in each function varies inversely with the costs of reproducing the skill required in that function and directly with the number of units using the product of the given function.

Differentiation of functions has its normative counterpart in inequalities among the units engaged in diverse functions. Inequality stems in part from differential access to environmental inputs and in part from differentials in costs of reproducing functional competences. On both counts unit claims on sustenance flows are uneven. Position in a relational sequence affects the priority ordering in the allocations of sustenance. And since reproducibility costs entail opportunity costs as well as costs born by the system, units seek compensations proportional to the benefits they have forgone in preparation for their respective functions.[7]

The model a system invariably assumes, therefore, is that of a hierarchically ordered set of functions. At the apex stands the key function, and below it are arrayed strata representing categories of contingent functions. The whole is an organization of power. That is, power is a system property; it is measured by the capacity of the system for the production of sustenance and for environmental control. But within the system, power is differentially distributed. Every function shares in the given amount of power in accordance with (a) its degree of removal from a direct environmental relationship and (b) the degree to which its specialization is reproducible. In general, power is disproportionately concentrated in the key function, and it diminishes as a function becomes further removed from direct environmental contact. The extent of specialization, however, affects the number of functions over which a given amount of power is spread. Thus, the greater the number of links in a chain of specializations, the more widely distributed is the power of a system and the smaller is the share, therefore, that can be exercised by each function. The power vested in the key function may be attenuated in the degree to which that function is divided among specialists.

Power, it should be noted, belongs to functions rather than to units. Units acquire power as they succeed to functions, and they lose it as they are displaced from functions. The implied distinction between functional and unit power is a useful one, for the two are not necessarily equal. They differ in the measure to which any given function is performed by more than one unit. If the power of a unit cannot exceed that of the function it performs, then unit power P' is equal to the power of a function P divided by the number of units N engaged in that function or $P' = P/N$. There is always the possibility of mobilizing distributed power. I shall take up that matter in a later section.

System Structure: The Commensalistic Sector

As pointed out in an earlier paragraph, the members of a population tend to engage in concerted action on the basis of similarities as well as differences. By engaging in uniform, parallel actions when faced with a common threat, a population can mobilize a formidable power. In that way it can rise in defense of its territory or of its symbiotic sector. By the same means it constitutes itself a polity with consensus on rules, procedures, and sanctions.

Homogeneity, however, is subdivisible almost without end. Just as each unit of a population is the possessor of a different combination of characteristics, so there may be many criteria of categorization employed in the system. Of these the most prominent and the most fundamental is that based on function (cf. Davis and Moore 1945). Functional differentiation sorts units into classes or strata that may be broadly or specifically defined. Sex and age are universally used as bases for the ascription of functions. These are supplemented in many instances by acquired occupational differentia that have no clear

correlation with biological characteristics. Apart from differentia of a functional sort, many more classificatory criteria,
such as lineage, ethnic background, region of birth, education,
past experiences, and other attributes too numerous to list,
may divide a population.

Every distinguishing characteristic possessed by two or
more units defines a potential for coaction, that is, such units
tend to engage in parallel actions performed more or less in
cadence. This is particularly noticeable among units that share
a given function, though it is observable in all other coacting
categories. The rhythmic occurrence of similar activities is
mutually reinforcing in several respects. I have already noted
that some tasks or the pursuit of some interests cannot be
accomplished in any other way. There is the further fact,
however, that the recurrence of like activities creates and preserves conditions essential to the conduct of each activity
taken separately. In the functional sphere a number of regularly performed acts produces a product sufficient in volume to
support the regular performance of other contingent functions. Accordingly, each functional unit derives a measure of
security from a number of coactors doing the same thing with
the same frequency. This is sometimes described as "critical
mass." Coaction is also a means of fostering other conditions
that are useful, if not essential, to the protection of a function
or, for that matter, of an interest of whatever kind. It is a means
of achieving consensus as to how an interest or a function
should be conducted and of acquiring the means for enforcing
its rules of procedure. How explicit that consensus becomes
depends on how specific is the definition of the category, how
concentrated are members of the category, and how frequently the members convene for joint action.

In summary, the commensal sector is composed of a number of categories of like-acting units that lie, as it were, hori-
zontally in the symbiotic hierarchy. Some may be very broadly
defined, others may be highly specific. Some lie entirely
within and are identified with a functional stratum, others
may cut across two or more strata. Although the sector may
have a structure composed of categories that persist through
time, it is also somewhat fluid. That is, the member units may
align themselves in different combinations from time to time,
as various characteristics become the objects of risk or threat.

Time and Space

Interdependence is constrained and shaped by the temporal limitations confronting the human organism. All activity is time-consuming, and all of it draws on a limited fund of time. Movement, the mechanism through which interdependence operates, must contend with other activities for a share of that fund. How much time must be allocated to communication and circulation depends on the number of functions present in the system and the frequencies with which they are carried on. An ecosystem is, among other things, a means of economizing on the uses of time.

One of the ways of achieving efficiency in the use of time is to assign classes of functions to different segments of a time span. Each class of functions then operates with a distinctive rhythm. Temporal spacing is regulated to a very large extent by the recurring needs for food and rest. But there are also other influencing factors. Normally the key function occupies the prime position in the time span of the diurnal cycle. All other functions are distributed with reference to the rhythm of the key function's operation. Functions concurrent in their complementarity share a given temporal position. Even so, each may exhibit a somewhat distinctive rhythm owing to the peculiarities of the function and of the way in which it complements related functions. The remaining functions are relegated to various temporal positions preceding or following that occupied by the key function. Uses of the "off-hours" in this way enhances the availability of functions to all members of the population. The many rhythms that may be represented in a system pose a need for their coordination that is only partly met by the differential distribution of functions through a diurnal period.

A second means of economizing on the uses of time is to delegate responsibility for movement and communication to classes of specialists, such as teamsters, messengers, road builders, transportation engineers, and the like. This does not occur usually until the time spaces become densely crowded with activities. It is then that specialized coordinators—timekeepers, dispatchers, and managers—make their appearance. But these specializations presuppose a relatively high level of productivity.

There is still another way in which time is conserved: by concentrating in relatively close proximity the units engaged in interrelated functions. As the distance separating functioning units is reduced, the time spent in transactions is also reduced, other things being constant. Thus human settlement is all but universally nucleated. The city is the preeminent example of interunit accessibility heightened by concentration.

In light of the foregoing, it is evident that space enters into human experience largely as a derivative of the time available for movement. Distance is measured in terms of the time that passes in the movement from point to point.[8] Likewise, area is apprehended as the amount of territory that can be cultivated, managed, or kept under surveillance within measured segments of time. Of course, territory has other properties, such as contours, vegetation, and resources. I am here referring merely to its dimensions, to the notion of space. In short, space is a function of time, and time, in turn, is defined by the way a system is constituted.

The Normative Order

An ecosystem in both its symbiotic and commensalistic sectors operates with a pulsating regularity. The system is manifested in repetitive actions; functions are recurring behaviors, and relationships are patterned interactions. Of necessity there is also a standardization of terms of discourse, of operating procedures, of means of dealing with contingencies, of ordering principles of various kinds. They constitute the measure of the integrity of a system. And that is a property of concern shared by all or most members of the population involved. It is a generalized mode of commensalism of which all other expressions are special cases.

This set of rhythmic and standardized ways of acting are expressive of the normative aspect of the system. A norm is represented in each instance of behavior to the extent that deviations from the pattern are few or of limited range. Rarely, however, can the norms be allowed to remain entirely unspoken. For the new cohorts must be instructed in the ways of the system, and individual deviations must be controlled. Accordingly, a substantial part of the behavioral repertory gains verbal expression as laws and codes of action. No doubt some are lifted to explicit formulation as a consequence of earlier challenges to established practice. Whatever may be the explanation of the accumulation of explicit statements of the rules of action, the normative system as verbalized should correspond closely to the routines of behavior, especially in an equilibrated system. This is not to imply that a behavior set composing a system must be fully meshed in a logically coherent and tightly integrated whole in either its substantive or its normative aspect. A system is capable of retaining a certain amount of contrary and disjunctive content. How much is an empirical question of considerable interest.

Some of the norms, because they have critical importance for the welfare of the whole, are endowed with a moral quality. They are judged to be true and good. Others, however, remain simply as rules of convenience. It is not unlikely that all rules fall on a continuum reaching from one extreme to the other. That aside, the two features of explicit formulation and moral inflection have led many observers to attribute to the normative code something akin to an independent existence. Talcott Parsons (1961), for one, attempts to conceptualize a social system exclusively in terms of verbalized norms. In doing so he assumes the risk of reifying an abstraction. Granted that it might be expedient on occasion to examine the normative code apart from its context, that should not be allowed to obscure the fact that rule and action are one and the same. Thus to the extent that closure has developed in a system, its normative order parallels and is expressive of the functional order.

Closure and Its Implications

The stability of a system rests in part on its degree of closure. Closure as applied to a living system can be no more than a relative concept, for no such system can exist independent of an environment. Closure is maximized, however, where the biophysical environment is paramount and where a key function monopolizes relations with the ecumenic environment. Under such conditions, environmental variations are for the most part noncumulative and productive of reversible effects.

A stable system is conceivably capable of homeostasis when the following conditions obtain. First, the functions performed are mutually complementary and sufficient to provide the operating conditions required by each. This assumes that all of the instrumental information at hand is fully utilized. Second, births and deaths are equal, and the age and sex distribution is stationary. That being the case, the number of units engaged in each function is just sufficient to maintain the relations of each function to all other functions comprising the system. New entrants to the labor force equal the number of departures from the labor force. Population size is thus optimal for the operation of the system. Third, the various functionally differentiated units are arranged in time and space such that the accessibility of each one to every other is directly related to the frequency of exchanges between them. This is to say that mobility costs present no barriers to the retrieval of available information and energy.

Whether the stable system may be regarded as constituting an equilibrium depends somewhat on whether equilibrium must be construed only in thermodynamic terms, that is, as attainable only under conditions of maximum entropy.[9] Unfortunately, equilibrium has suffered considerable misuse, notably in the assumption that it constitutes an ideal state. Yet some notion of proportionality, balance, or coherence is eminently useful as a benchmark against which to compare variations. Equilibrium may thus be used to convey the notion of a steady state.

A reasonable question is therefore: How realistic is an equilibrium concept as applied to a relatively isolated ecosystem engaged in a self-sufficient environmental relationship? Various scholars have affirmed the realism of such a concept. According to Dumond (1975, 714), whose approach is from a demographic perspective, "The model that must be adopted for early humanity is one in which natality is in approximate balance with mortality from natural and routine external causes, in which the stable population is well within the normal carrying capacity of the region, and yet in which a margin of fecundity . . . somehow exists as a necessary safety mechanism." Fisher (1971, 4) believes that such a system can remain stable for centuries. For neither subsistence production nor production for small markets encourages growth of the division of labor. Likewise, Wilkinson (1973, 19) contends that a variety of prehistoric and historic societies have developed conditions necessary for stability. A more restrained view is expressed by Bennett (1976, 12), who sees an equilibrium state as but a pause in the evolutionary tendency toward exponential increases in environmental impact.

It is more than likely, to repeat a point made earlier, that equilibrium is at best an average condition. The technological deprivation associated with isolation and self-sufficiency leaves a local group with a rather tenuous control over its environment. Seasonal variations in rainfall and temperatures, cycles in the survival rates of predators and pests, and vagaries of intergroup relations produce swings of varying amplitudes in the food supply. These have their effects on vital rates, on the number of people available for the performance of traditional tasks, and on the ability of the group to continue the practice of its folkways. Still, if system structure is reasserted after each departure from a central tendency, it may be said that equilibrium prevails.

Granted the occurrence in fact of systems in steady state, the model as outlined in these paragraphs is designed mainly for heuristic purposes. Its utility lies in its identification of the properties of a system that are most sensitive to influences leading to cumulative change.

Propositional Résumé

The preceding discussion may be summarized in the following assumptions and hypotheses:

Assumptions

2-A1　Population tends to fill all resource space available in the organization of an ecosystem.

2-A2　Adaptation is a collective behavior process.

2-A3　Collective (adaptive) behavior revolves around two axes, one symbiotic, the other commensalistic, both of which serve as bases for the distribution of environmental access.

2-A4　An ecosystem appears when environmental access is partitioned such that one or two functions become responsible for mediating a critical environmental relationship for all other functions.

2-A5 The necessity for environmental access confers a determining influence upon the means for transportation and communication in the acquisition and accumulation of all other elements of technology.

Hypotheses

2-H1 The function that mediates the critical environmental relationship regulates the conditions under which all other functions are performed.

2-H2 The emergence of a key function arrays all other functions in series by degree of removal from direct access to environment.

2-H3 The greater the differentiation of functions, the greater is the proportion of all functions that are indirectly related to environment.

2-H4 The number of units (population) engaged in each function varies inversely with the cost of reproducing the skill used in the function and directly with the number of units using the product of the given function.

2-H5 In any given state of mobility costs, a temporal ordering of differentiated functions appears which reflects the respective needs for environmental access and the frequency of exchanges with other functions.

2-H5.1 A temporal order is manifested as a spatial order.

2-H6 Power in an ecosystem is disproportionately concentrated in the key function and diminishes with each degree of removal from direct access to environment.

2-H7 Stability through time in the number of and the interrelations among functions (closure) varies directly with mobility costs.

2-H8 Under conditions of closure, a normative order parallels the functional order.

3

Ecosystem Change:

The Concept

In the preceding chapter a conception of an ecosystem in the form of a steady-state equilibrium was presented. That was done partly for descriptive convenience, but also to identify variables to be observed under conditions of change. The use of such a model as a heuristic device has ample precedent (Parsons 1949). The danger in such a tactic, of course, lies in the risk of confusing the model with reality. Presumably an intensive examination of change is a sufficient protection against falling victim to that hazard.

The Meaning of Change

Change is commonly regarded as an irreversible and non-repetitive alteration of an object. Irreversibility may be due, as A. J. Lotka (1924) has pointed out, to a simple improbability that elements, when moved about randomly, can be immediately returned to their original order. But it may also be due to the creation of new variables in the course of modification. For one or another of these reasons an object is changed when it cannot be restored to its initial state. If it reverts to a more primitive condition, it must follow a different path from that traversed in attaining its present form.

The object of change for purposes of this volume is the ecosystem viewed as a unitary phenomenon. What constitutes change in an ecosystem is implicit in the definition of a system stated in the preceding chapter. That is, change occurs as a shift in the number and kinds of functions or as a rearrangement of functions in different combinations. Usually the occurrence of one involves the occurrence of the other. Simple though they may seem, such alterations have profound repercussions. They affect the number of people who are needed and who can be supported, the techniques and tools that can be used, the disposition of system parts in time and space, and the composition of the normative code.

Excluded from the conception of change as used here are internal variations that have no sequels and cyclical fluctuations that are intrinsic to the functioning of a system. A family, for example, might modify its internal routines without affecting its relations with complementing units. Or a given unit might disappear and be replaced by another similar unit without disturbing a set of relationships. Similarly, day and night alterations, the seasonal round, the life cycle, the succession of generations sow no seeds of change, though they are among the points where the visibility of change, when it occurs, is greatest.

The Origins of Change

There are two seemingly opposed views of the origins of system change. One contends that change is internally induced; the other holds change to be the result of external influences generated in the environment. Whether change is continuous or discontinuous is also a point of some disagreement.

The classic conception of change as an internally caused process was put forth by Karl Marx. In his view, change is produced by internal contradictions that develop primarily between the "forces of production" (i.e., technology) and the "relations of production" (i.e., the organization of production). Whereas the forces of production are cumulative, the relations of production are relatively inert (1904, 21). The multiplication of contradictions builds an increasing pressure upon a prevailing equilibrium until the existing relations of production are dissolved and a new set of relations of production is established (1967, 3:249). Marx provided no clues as to how or by what means the forces of production accumulate. That appears to have been accepted as a given.

Pitirim Sorokin also espoused an internal causation of change (1941, chap. 12). But unlike Marx, who regarded change as a discontinuous process, Sorokin thought of change as continuous. Change, he said, is immanent. It proceeds though the accretion of infinitely small alterations. Although he recognized that external influences might be facilitating, Sorokin insisted that systems change even in fixed environments (1947, 696–700). He provided no exposition, however, of how change was produced.

Wilbert Moore (1963) offers a more analytical explication of internally caused change. He finds its basis in the improbability of exact reproducibility of role behavior on the part of successive occupants of positions, in the genetic variability of successive cohorts, and in the interruptions in the staffing of roles that result from a more or less random mortality. There is therefore an inherent instability in a system that generates a creeping change leading eventually to significant cumulative effects. Moore's argument is not convincing, however. His contention that stability or continuity presupposes exact reproducibility from moment to moment begs the question, though that is a position encouraged by "functionalism." That there can be flexibility without change should need little argument. Flexibility is the guarantor of continuity. If a system were unable to tolerate minor variations in the relations among its parts, it would be threatened with destruction by every disturbance that occurred. But since disturbances are often temporary and impinge on no more than a particular relationship or sector, a system is able to return to its original state with no lasting effects. An important question concerning this as well as other aspects of structure has to do with the amount of tolerance for variation that exists in a system.

The conception of change as dependent on external influences recognizes an inescapable system-environment interaction. It rests, moreover, on both logical and empirical foundations. Logically it is impossible for a thing to cause itself. On the empirical side, scholars in many disciplines have observed the critical importance of environmental inputs for system change (Toynbee 1956, 59–60; Lewis 1957; Braudel 1966, 161; Rostow 1960, 6; Stevenson 1968; Swanson 1971; Utterbach 1974; Baldridge and Burnham 1975). This is not to say that a system is a passive factor in a change process. On the contrary, it contains elements that facilitate as well as obstruct change-inducing events.

Where there is a reluctance to accept the external origins position, it rests in part on a failure to observe a distinction between what are called, in Aristotelian language, efficient and material causes. No external event A (efficient cause), let us say, can produce effect Y in the absence of certain system properties $a, a', a'', \ldots$ (material causes). On the other hand, the mere presence of properties $a, a', a'', \ldots$ will not lead to effect Y unless event A has been brought to bear on the system. That there may be feedback effects from $a, a', a'', \ldots$ to A is no contradiction of the above hypothesis; such effects merely complicate the cause-and-effect relationship.

Another source of resistance to the external origins principle of changes lies in our having lost sight of the linkages among happenings, which is easy to do when dealing with complex phenomena. A new influence usually impinges first and most forcibly on a particular segment of a system. Change in that segment is subsequently transmitted to other related segments in a concatenation of effects that might be spread over an extended period of time. Unless the whole sequence is known, it appears that change in any one segment originated within the system. The observational task posed by the sequential transmission of effects is obviously not a simple one. In instances in which a student is interested only in change in a particular segment of a system, it might not be worth the effort to trace the series of effects back to its beginnings. But that would be a decision based on expedience, not on principle. The danger of being led into an infinite regress by the external origins principle is not a serious one. How far one need retreat to earlier events to locate the exogenous factor is indicated in the definition of the unit in which change is being observed.

Perhaps the greatest difficulty encountered in applying the external origins principle rests with the inside-outside distinction that must be made. Phenomena that are amorphously bounded, as are many ecosystems, seem to lack the assumed unit character. I have minimized this difficulty by starting with an equilibrium model. But that, of course, is a heuristic fiction. Most ecosystems are open systems, and some are loose congeries of partially integrated subsystems. In such instances it is difficult to locate effective boundaries, though the issue can often be resolved by definition. As a general rule, the more closely a system approximates a unity, the greater is the necessity that change originate from external disturbances (see Goldschmidt 1959; Nisbet 1969; Rostow 1960; Wolfe 1957, 7). It should be noted, however, that immanent change offers no escape from the boundary problem, for it posits an interior in which change is alleged to be generated.

What has been presented as two opposing views of change makes much more sense if regarded as complementary phases of a single process. That is, social system change is resolvable into internal and external phases. The internal phase, which constitutes the more protracted segment, consists in drawing out the implications of accumulated information. By arranging and rearranging elements of knowledge in various combinations a series of deductions and inductions, that is, discoveries or inventions, is derived. Conceivably such a process continues until all or nearly all combinations of existing knowledge have been explored. As that point is approached, the rate of internal change subsides and equilibrium conditions begin to appear. The time required to reach such a state varies with the amount of accumulated knowledge. That, in turn, may be contingent on various other circumstances. Those will be discussed in a later section.

A resumption of the process of change requires the acquisition of new items of information, either as novel forms of behavior or as behavior abstracted to constitute information. Such acquisitions can occur only as inputs from the system's environment. Thus is added an element that can be tried in various combinations with old elements in a search for workable inferences. As those appear, an equilibrium is dissolved and a system moves through another internal phase to a new state. The latter does not happen without the input from the outside, without the external phase of change.

The interaction of internal with external phases of change is manifested in various ways. Quite often the occupance and use of a habitat by a resettled population will so modify habitat conditions that the occupying group cannot continue a given mode of life indefinitely in that location. Use might alter the soil content through repeated plantings of a single food crop without fertilization, provoke erosion by affecting the drainage pattern, or create conditions that attract new kinds of predators. Unless the group gains new information that enables it to restore habitat productivity, it will have to migrate or suffer a progressive attrition in sustenance supply with all that implies for survival. This was the outcome of cotton cultivation in the southeastern United States. Another instance of feedback effect occurs where equilibrated systems maintain themselves by expelling the surplus members of each generation. If the expelled members devise ways of surviving in the vicinity of the familiar habitat, they become a new element in the environment of the parent system. The dispossessed sons of landed families in medieval Europe, for example, became brigands, mercenary soldiers, and merchants, all potentially important bearers of novelty.

Many variations that occur in the biophysical environment, such as day-to-day temperature fluctuations, small alterations of the growing season, or rises and falls in populations of parasites, may have little or no effect. Ecosystems generally possess enough resilience to absorb the effects of small oscillations in their environments without experiencing structural changes. Even an extreme deviation from the normal, if it is of short duration, may leave no permanent mark on a system. But where one or more functions are rendered inoperative by physical or biotic shifts, the system may have to be reconstituted in a different pattern. The disappearance of a game supply, the silting of an estuary, or a volcanic eruption can force a move to a different habitat and a renewal of adaptive efforts to deal with a new set of conditions. In that event, the system reforms around a modified key function. If no new information has been acquired, the system may regress to a simpler form. But the biophysical environment is not of itself productive of information.

Exposure to an ecumenic environment has vastly greater implications. From it are transmitted influences having both additive and multiplicative effects. A site on a traveled road is directly accessible to an ecumenic environment; a location at an intersection of routes is open to a much wider ecumene. Earlier the ecumenic environment was characterized as an interaction field. In its primitive form the field is composed of a number of relatively independent systems, varying in size, resources, and accessibility of location. The origin of such a field doubtlessly lay in repeated occasions of overpopulation and group fission, followed by colonization of adjacent territories. The process, recently described by Sahlins (1958) and Carniero (1970), is actually as old as the history of human sedentary settlement. With the spread of settlement units, a network of routes of travel develops. Travelers, moving through the network carrying ideas, artifacts, and accounts of experiences, serve inadvertently thereby as agents of change. Information piles up, as it were, in the system with a strategic location in the network and drifts outward from there to systems with less favorable locations. Ecumenes, however, can be so insular as to be sheltered from external influences. Lambert (1964) attributes the relatively static character of Indian society to extreme segmentation. While there are many intervillage networks, none is inclusive and few bridge urban and rural segments. Only where a unit in a network occupies a site on a well-traveled road is there apt to be a resumption of cumulative change.

The occurrence of change-producing events tends to be random. There may be uncertainty in respect to the content, the frequency, and the order of appearance of items of information conveyed along communication paths. Much of the information is apt to be trivial or irrelevant to the capabilities of a given system. It may include gossip, hearsay, fragments of information, erroneous facts, and inappropriate technical lore. There can also be great variation in the frequency with which useful items appear in the information flow; in some periods they might be widely spaced in time, while in others they might follow in rapid succession. Again, some information that might be useful under certain conditions lacks that value because it occurs in the wrong sequence. Sometimes such information is lost for want of an adequate information storage facility; in others it may be unused long after the missing pieces have been acquired because the means of information retrieval are underdeveloped. In general, the random composition of information flows points to the necessity of thinking of the incidence of change-producing influences in probabilistic terms.

The probability of cumulative change is raised where the information acquired is converted to means of reducing the costs of movement, that is, improving the techniques of trans-

portation and communication.[1] Incremental effects of information flows, however, can be highly uneven, if mechanical and
organizational components of technology do not occur in fairly
close sequence. Technological history includes many instances of mechanical inventions that have remained dormant
for decades and longer for want of an appropriate organization
for their use.[2]

The Modes of Change: Growth

The second and third propositions set forth in the paradigm in
chapter 2 distinguish growth from evolution. By *growth* is
meant the maturation of a system through the maximization of
the potential for complexity and integration implicit in the
technology for movement and communication possessed at a
given point in time. *Evolution*, on the other hand, refers to the
occurrence of new structural elements resulting from environmental inputs that lead to syntheses of new with old information and a consequent increase in the scope of the accessible
environment. The one is a development of inherent or latent
potential; the other is the creation of a higher order of potential.[3]

System growth is assumed to follow a typical pattern that
corresponds to an S-shaped or logistic curve, which results
from differential rates of change as between critical variables or
parameters of a system. Change in the more dynamic variable
uses up the support capacity of the more slowly changing
variable and comes to rest at an asymptote or equilibrium point
fixed by the latter variable. This generalized growth model was
given mathematical expression by Pearl and Verhulst as

$$\frac{dx}{dt} = rx\left(1 - \frac{x}{k}\right),$$

where x is the number of units comprising a system, t is time, r
is rate of change, and k is the factor that determines the number of units of which a system can be composed, often described as carrying capacity.

A number of observations concerning this highly simplified
model need to be made. The first concerns the two growth
phases represented in the curve. The phase of accelerating

change pertains to the period in a system's history of rapid organizational growth. In that phase the amount of energy recoverable for use from the energy taken into the system is steadily increased. The decelerating phase marks an approach to an end to growth of order, together with a stabilization of the proportion of recoverable energy. Increases in negative entropy give way to decreases as an asymptote is neared (Bertalanffy 1952, 113; Buckley 1967, 51). Should organization tend to grow beyond the point of maximum recoverable energy, entropy becomes positive. Presumably at that point a system tends to return to scale.

The term *succession* is used in bioecology to denote the growth process (Clements 1916; Odum 1969). It is possible, at least so far as the plant association is concerned, to identify a series of well-marked stages, each of which comprises a distinctive association of species. The series concludes with a final or climax stage at which the communal or ecosystem is in equilibrium with its environment. But the human ecologist has not been able to identify an analogous ontogenetic series for the human ecosystem (Park 1936b). Nor is it likely to prove possible, according to Cain, who contends that "history in its description of the rise, culmination, and decline of civilizations, is antithetical to the concepts of succession and climax" (1960, 160). But that view is, on the one hand, a fragmentary perspective of history and, on the other hand, a too rigid conception of succession. In fact, the older view of succession as an iterative series of stages ending in a climax stage has been abandoned by bioecologists (Pickett 1976, 109). Current use of the concept defines it as a movement of a system toward an asymptote, given no change in environment (Margalef 1968, 28–29). That conception is nearly identical with the growth concept as defined in these pages.

A third observation of the simple model has to do with the determination of carrying capacity. Its application of the Malthusian argument may be suitable for plants and animals, but its transfer to the human species is highly questionable, as Karl Marx was among the first to point out (1936, 68ff.). It reckons without an understanding of ecosystem structure and of how it changes. Where an ecosystem is unchanging through relatively long periods of time, it may appear that the biophysical environment limits the amount of growth possible. That, however, is an illusion resulting from a confusion of stability with an absence of causation. An ecosystem, other things constant, contains its own limits to growth, and those limiting conditions come into operation independent of the composition of the biophysical environment. I shall return to this proposition for a closer look in chapter 6.

A growth cycle is most readily observable where critical inputs from an environment are so widely spaced in time that the potential implicit in each can be more or less fully extracted and incorporated in a system's structure before the next critical input occurs. This appears to have been the kind of experience that culminated in each of the many instances of protracted stability recorded in historical and anthropological literature. Various explanations of such an outcome have been proposed. Turner's (1940, 2:1928) suggestion, cast in terms of a limited food supply, echoes the Malthusian argument. Somewhat similar is Elvin's (1973, 19) proposal that growth ceases when the technological potential is counterbalanced by the burden of size. But Quigley (1961) contends that limits are reached when surplus wealth is diverted from innovation to the maintenance of bureaucracy. There is then an onset of closure.

The Modes of Change: Evolution

Where, however, an established equilibrium is disrupted and a system is moved to a higher level of complexity, it appears that the elements of an evolutionary model are present. Repetitions of that process may form a sequence of growth alternating with equilibrium. Applications of the growth cycle conception, as in the earlier ethnological literature, led to a classificatory treatment of change as a series of evolutionary stages. Morgan's (1877) formulation of social evolution as a progression from savagery to barbarism to civilization is of that order. A more sophisticated use of the classificatory treatment is found in Goldschmidt's (1959, 183) series of stages ranging from nomadic hunting and gathering, through settled hunting and gathering, horticultural, agricultural-state, and finally to industrial-state society. Goldschmidt was fully aware, however, of gradations of difference between stages.

The sequence-of-stages concept of evolution has been subject to criticism for the arbitrariness involved in defining stages. That there is substance to such criticisms is evident from a close examination of particular cases. The history of transportation and communication, for example, appears to fall into three stages based on sources of energy utilized: animal, mechanical, and electronic. For millennia, ending some time after the appearance of the tacking sail (tenth century) and the magnetic compass (fifteenth century), mobility was powered exclusively by animal and human muscular strength. The mechanically powered epoch, clearly launched with the innovations that made open-sea sailing possible, received an enormous impetus with the development of the steam engine, in the nineteenth century, and again with the later appearance of the internal combustion engine. Nevertheless, the use of animal-powered mobility continued well into the twentieth century, particularly for local movements. Beginning in the 1830s with the introduction of the telegraph, the reliance on electronically powered means of overcoming time and distance has progressed at an accelerated pace and is still far from realizing its full potential. Again, a large overlap of regimes exists, for mechanically powered means of transporting people and goods still prevail, despite enormous advances in electronic technology. Apart from its speed and versatility, the latter had a revolutionary importance in its separation of communication from transportation.

In short, the identification of stages in the change process is usually moot; where one begins and ends is almost always debatable. A response to that stricture is that technological eras cannot be created de novo. It is to be expected that old practices will persist into new technological epochs. The stage distinction hinges upon the degree of predominance of one form or indicator of organization over another. Needless to say, the measure used must be clearly defined and demonstrable. If that requirement is satisfied, the stage conception can be an effective descriptive tool, particularly for converting historic to analytical time.

The classificatory stage sequence approach has also suffered from its failure to disclose the mechanics of the evolution process. One attempts to deal with that omission is provided in the widely accepted biological model. Briefly stated, that model is based on the phenomena of individual variation and environmental selection. Variation occurs with the appearance of mutant forms resulting from one or another kind of interbreeding. Given the presence of variation, selection operates to affect the survival probabilities of the mutants.[4] A pressure for selection develops where the number of individuals exceeds the capacity of a niche to accommodate the entire population of progeny. Competition ensues, and individuals unsuited for the parental niche are forced to look elsewhere for a niche to which the mutant characteristics are fitted. If successful, selection may be said to have taken place. The new niche might be found in the parental system or in an alien system. In either case the receiving system must be an open one. A closed system offers no opportunities for niche creation. There remains a question, however, whether an excess population can alone so disrupt an equilibrium that closure gives way to openness.[5]

The application of the biological model to the evolution of the human ecosystem calls for a number of translations. In the first place, information items must be treated as analogous to genes (Boulding 1978, 32–34; Lenski and Lenski 1982, 57), though it is not apparent that the same principle governs the intermingling of genes with genes and information with information. Moreover, since genetic variations, or mutants, issue as new species, assuming survival, a counterpart for species in the human ecosystem must be identified. Should it be an informational synthesis, for example, an invention, a differentiated segment of the population (e.g., an occupation), or a new subsystem? A further question arises in connection with selection. In the biological model the biophysical environment is regarded as the selective agent. But that not only denies any power of selectivity in the organism, it confuses two possible selecting agents. If we detach the biotic element from the physical element, we find we have separated a dynamic from a passive component. The biotic element, even at the simple organizational level, is usually, if not invariably, organized as a network of relations among species, that is, an ecosystem. It would seem clear, therefore, that the dynamic potential combined with the niche structure of the system constitute it as the selective agent.[6] Thus a strong case can be made for a Lamarckian as against a Darwinian model of evolution. This argument applies with no less force to the human ecosystem. It is subject to impingements from its ecumenic environment, including items of information, skill-bearing immigrants, or units of organization, which occur in no necessary order. The affected system receives and assimilates some items and turns others aside. It does that not out of any teleological propensity. A system's degree of integration determines the efficiency of its selection, though perhaps at some cost to the likelihood of evolutionary advance. Mistakes can occur, some with devastating consequences. There is no necessity that a system should survive. But it does not follow from externality and randomness of occurrence of change-inducing influences that system change is without direction, as Nisbet (1969) has contended. The fact that change proceeds by stops and starts does not alter its cumulative character.

The more fundamental problem with the evolution model as applied to the human ecosystem concerns the logic of transferring a phylogenetic process to an ontogenetic phenomenon. That ecosystem "ontogeny recapitulates phylogeny" has not been established. In the present state of knowledge it seems more reasonable to expect the evolution of human ecosystems to follow multilinear paths (Steward 1955). This notion occupies a middle position between history with its conception of unique chronologies and a single, embracive, unidirectional process of change. It recognizes that when changes are introduced into widely separated, unrelated systems, their effects unfold in different sequences. Whether the various paths of change converge upon a single course and under what conditions they might do so are questions of importance to a general theory of human ecology.[7]

The observational task of distinguishing between the two modes of change—growth and evolution—becomes progressively more difficult as the rate of change accelerates. Each approach to an asymptotic limit tends to be offset and obscured by new syntheses of acquisitions from the environment with existing system elements. This has lent support to an approach to change as a continuum in which growth and evolution are merged (Carniero and Tobias 1963; Freeman and Winch 1957; Schwartz and Miller 1964). A recent application of that notion was developed by Frisbie and Clark (1979). They constructed a multiple-factor index of technology and used it as an independent variable in a regression analysis with economic growth, urbanization, political modernization, bureaucratization, and phase in the demographic transition as dependent variables. Their results provided support for the continuum view of change, as well as showing a strong explanatory power of technology. This, however, does not fully dispose of the problem of operationally separating growth and evolution. It is quite possible for variation on one parameter to be arrested while variations on other parameters continue in process. Still that could be an illusion due to failure to clearly define an ecosystem's boundaries. All of which is to say that while growth and evolution are conceptually distinguishable, their separation for observational purposes calls for explicit statement of the measures to be used. Therein lies the crux of the problem. The temptation to retreat to a conception of evolution as simply an increase in complexity is understandable therefore. Or as Margalef has stated the matter, succession (i.e., growth) is inherent in ecosystems, and evolution is drawn along encased in succession's frame (1968). In view of the difficult observational problems, it seems prudent to collapse growth and evolution in the concept of cumulative change.

A System Change Model

The notion of change developed in the following chapters is depicted in the system change model (fig. 1). In that exhibit exogenous influences are shown to be impinging upon an equilibrium state. The consequent disequilibrium passes through first-order and later second-order effects, the latter moving from general to more specific outcomes. As the specific conditions of disequilibrium develop, they open the door wider to exogenous influences. That feedback allows cumulative change to accelerate. A tendency toward a return to equilibrium, manifested in the subsiding of population growth, is offset by rapid accumulation of information and a continuing reduction of mobility costs.

PROPOSITIONAL RÉSUMÉ

Assumption

3-A1 Ecosystem change originates from external influences and proceeds through syntheses of external inputs with internal properties.

FIG. 1. SYSTEM CHANGE MODEL

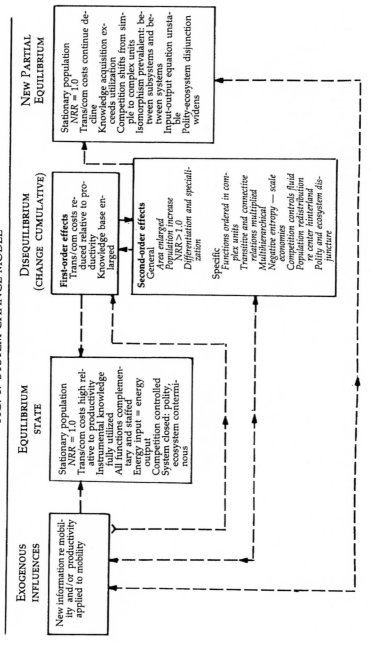

EXOGENOUS INFLUENCES

New information re mobility and/or productivity applied to mobility

EQUILIBRIUM STATE

Stationary population
NRR = 1.0
Trans/com costs high relative to productivity
Instrumental knowledge fully utilized
All functions complementary and staffed
Energy input = energy output
Competition controlled
System closed: polity, ecosystem conterminous

DISEQUILIBRIUM (CHANGE CUMULATIVE)

First-order effects
Trans/com costs reduced relative to productivity
Knowledge base enlarged

Second-order effects
General
Area enlarged
Population increase
NRR > 1.0
Differentiation and specialization

Specific
Functions ordered in complex units
Transitive and connective relations multiplied
Multihierarchical
Negative entropy — scale economies
Competition controls fluid
Population redistribution re center hinterland
Polity and ecosystem disjuncture

NEW PARTIAL EQUILIBRIUM

Stationary population
NRR = 1.0
Trans/com costs continue decline
Knowledge acquisition exceeds utilization
Competition shifts from simple to complex units
Isomorphism prevalent: between subsystems and between systems
Input-output equation unstable
Polity-ecosystem disjunction widens

Hypotheses

3-H1 The greater the exposure to influences from an ecumenic environment, the greater the probability of change.

3-H2 Ecosystem change occurs as new information is converted to new functions (specialization) or increased specialization of old functions.

3-H.1 Changes in specialization involve changes in relationships among functions.

3-H.2 Changes in the organization of relationships accompany mechanical innovations.

3-H3 Ecosystem change is cumulative when new information improves mobility directly or indirectly by applying increased productivity to mobility improvements.

3.H3.1 Efficiency of transportation and communication technology sets limits to complexity of ecosystem.

3-H4 Whenever differential rates of change occur among critical variables, the more rapidly changing variable moves through a logistic curve toward an asymptote fixed by the slower-changing variable.

3-H5 An approach to an asymptote in cumulative change in an ecosystem assumes a state of closure relative to ecumenic environment.

4

Cumulative Change:

Growth and Evolution

of the Ecosystem

Any increment in the information flow from the ecumenic environment offsets tendencies toward equilibrium. Disequilibrium becomes general in a system when the information increments produce cumulative effects. Thus a system moves from a state of near closure to openness. *Openness*, as used here, means the existence of more than one avenue of contact with the ecumene and, by implication, a responsiveness to inputs from that source. It does not mean complete vulnerability to environmental variations. Should that come about, the system would disappear in chaos. Open systems persist as such by virtue of the interlocking relations among complementary functions. Consequently, change can be neither random nor instantaneous. Change elements are transmitted along chains of functions in a process that is spread over time.

The point or points of entry into a system of environmental influences depends on the degree of integration among the parts. In a relatively closed system, the key function is the principle, if not the only, gateaway through which environmental influences may enter.[1] The unit in the role is in a position to exercise discretionary power over what may be selected. In a loosely integrated or open system, on the other hand, change elements can enter at any of several points.

Those may lie at the margins as well as at the center. There is a demographic margin as well as a territorial one. That is, an open system may lack well-marked paths along which youthful cohorts may move into full participation in a division of labor. Having few occupational habits, vested interests, and commitments of tradition, youthful cohorts tend to serve as vehicles of change (Ryder 1965).

System change, to repeat a definition, occurs when new functions are added and rearrangements among functions follow. The question of concern in this chapter has to do with the mechanisms of system change.

Disequilibrium

First-order effects of information inputs from an ecumenic environment are of two kinds. Most critical are reductions in the costs of transportation and communication. Savings in time spent in point-to-point movement result from increased applications of resources and energy to roadways and vehicles and to the organization for their use and maintenance. A second effect is the accumulation of knowledge. That presupposes a means of storage of a knowledge repertory. The preeminent storage facility, of course, is writing. But a mechanical tool also represents a storage device; every use of a tool is a retrieval of information. The two first-order effects are interactive. Reduced costs of movement facilitate the accumulation of information, and information accumulation increases the probability of further reductions of mobility costs.

Second-order effects of a general character are threefold. They, too, can be disentangled only for analytical purposes. They are (1) an enlargement of accessible area and resource base, (2) an increase of population, and (3) differentiation and specialization of functions.

Territory and Population

The enlargement of territory might begin simply as easier movement over an ecumene. Soon, however, the scope of accessible area is extended to the limits afforded by the improved facilities for movement. Territorial expansion raises the probability of increased variety and amounts of materials for the making of artifacts and for the nourishment of population. That some extension might enclose territory unusable in a prevailing state of technology for routine movements with existing transport facilities argues for a probabilistic view toward the outcome of expansion. Yet without territorial enlargement, increases in material supplies are unlikely, particularly in the early phase of cumulative change. Under primitive conditions of transport, expansion may require sovereign control of the added space to assure access. But as transport techniques are improved, the need for sovereign control diminishes, for access is achieved through indirect means to an increasing extent.

Increases in material supplies, especially food, whether due to applications of new land-use methods or to enlargements of accessible land, allow population to increase. The increase begins as a decline of the death rate and is manifested as an increase in the net reproduction or replacement rate. Thus each new cohort of births exceeds the number in the preceding cohort as long as the fertility rate remains higher than the mortality rate. The resulting growth of population supplies the personnel needed for advances in system complexity, while the correlated decline in average age enhances the adaptability potential in a population. A subsequent decline of fertility and an approach once again to a replacement rate at unity brings an end to growth through natural increase.[2]

Natural increase is not, however, the only means of increase in a system's population. Increases can come about much more rapidly through additions of occupied territory to the scope of a system. The absorption of outlying population tends to be progressive, advancing with the adjustment of the system to the new scale opened to it. Although the quantitative importance of the population increments gained in that way presents difficult measurement problems, such increments can be just as real and effective as increments gained in any other way. In fact, in late stages of system development, gains in effective population through extensions of access to wider territories become increasingly important, even to the point of substituting for other processes.

A third source of growth of population is through migration. Occasions when resources for system development are increased more rapidly than population interareal transfers

tend to occur, given a disturbance of a demographic equilibrium, in an area of migrant origin. The failure of the territorial
distribution of opportunities induced by system change to
match the prechange distribution of population occurs within
as well as between regions. Many an early town has lost its
eminence in production and trade as technological change and
new industries have favored other locations. In principle, intraregional migrations are not unlike interregional migrations.

It has been taken as axiomatic that, if an entity is to retain
unit character, increases in size require changes in form.[3] That
way of stating the matter may be suitable for physical entities;
but where ecosystems are concerned, changes in form may
operate as the independent factor as often as changes in
population size. Or rather, change in neither one can advance
far without corresponding change in the other. In any given
state of system organization there is an optimum population
size from which no more than small deviations can be tolerated
without serious consequences.[4] Therefore, the influence of
population size of necessity figures prominently in all propositions concerning system change. In fact, changes in population size constitute highly sensitive indicators of system
change. It should be borne in mind in regard to this and all
subsequent uses of population that I am referring exclusively
to an organized or systemic population.

Differentiation and Specialization

Third among the second-order effects of improved mobility
and information accumulation are differentiation and specialization. The process operates upon a relatively undifferentiated set of tasks performed by a simple unit, an individual.
The process begins whenever the number of units utilizing a
service or product yielded by a given task reaches a size sufficient to support a unit in the full-time performance of that
task. Specialization, said Adam Smith (1937, 17; see also Stigler
1957), varies with the extent of the market, that is, size of
population. In the definition of *market scope*, size of population
and territorial extent are not readily separable.[5]

The progress of specialization parallels fairly closely the
refinement of technology. Appearing first among industries
conducted in household units and using simple hand tools

and the materials native to a habitat, specialization is confined to local areas and subsists on exchanges through bartering. Market expansion stimulates increases in volume of production and the cultivation of special abilities. A concentration of effort on particular skills is both cause and effect of the development of specialized tools suited to the practice of the respective skills. In late stages of specialization by skill, occupations leave the household for regrouping in extra-household units. Further enlargements of markets, together with the universe of discourse, encourage ever-larger scale of production, more elaborate tools, and a fragmentation of skills into tasks.

Each step along the progression from industries to skills to tasks lengthens chains of symbiotic linkages and elaborates hierarchical structures. Functions are ordered in vertical sequences and in lateral arrays. The one is an extension of a given hierarchy; the other lays the groundwork for the rearing of hierarchies in one or more complementary functional spheres. The within-hierarchy specialization is a division of labor in production. The between-hierarchy specialization is a supplementation, or service, to production. Actually the conventional classification of functions as production and service, presumably based on their yielding tangible and intangible products, is arbitrary. Both classes of functions contribute to production; they differ in degree of directness involved in production. Production in one hierarchy is service to another.

Differentiation proceeds at the expense of a broadly based commensalism, while creating numerous opportunities for the formation of new, more specific commensal relations. Traditional mutual aid arrangements, founded usually on kin or tribal allegiances embracing common marital rules and religious observances, are eroded and threatened with extinction by new occupational alignments and a plethora of avocational vistas. It would be a mistake, however, to infer that atrophy of an inclusive relationship and the substitution of specialized functions often linked through one or more intervening functions, means any attenuation of interdependence. Anonymity among units does not lessen the necessity of one for the other. But differentiation in the commensal sphere does allow a relatively large degree of independence, if only because many such relations have no vital importance.

Specialization tends always to advance to the maximum

permitted by mobility costs, assuming a population size sufficient to staff the various functions and the possession of the requisite technology, conditions that are themselves contingent on mobility costs. The process releases population from labor intensive functions and makes it available for the fuller use of a technical repertory, that is, further advances of specialization. As the units engaged in specialized functions are necessarily spread over space, their exchanges draw from a limited fund of time and energy upon which all other activities depend. Consequently, only so much of that fund, other things constant, can be allocated to any given class of activity, for example, transportation and communication, without impairing the conduct of other classes of activity. For that reason there is a ceiling to the extent of differentiation supportable at any one moment. It follows, therefore, that reductions in mobility costs lift the ceiling to a higher level and allow further progress in specialization.

A necessary correlative to differentiation is standardization of the conditions under which functions are performed. A generalization of use value of the product of each function, at least to the extent needed for continuous support of the function, is of course a first requirement. This assumes common terms of discourse, including verbal symbols, weights and measures, and coinage. So simple a standardizing innovation as the single price for commodity purchases, which began to displace the old bartering practice late in the nineteenth century, enormously facilitated the conduct of transactions. Standardization, in short, is a reduction of mobility costs.

The importance of political centralization in the propagation of standardization can hardly be overemphasized. The suppression of brigandage, the uniform application of criteria of justice, the protection of coinage, the elimination of tolls on highways and streams, and the development of a unified road system await the appearance of a central administrative power. And with its emergence, standardization passes into civility. No complex system can long survive where individuals do not accord to strangers as well as to kinsmen the rights they claim for themselves. Civility advances with the decline of kinship autonomy and of parochialism of whatever kind.[6]

The appearance of each added function gives rise to two, three, or more relationships. Every functionally specialized unit must maintain relations with a clientele, with complementary producing units, and with various service units. Differentiation of functions also fosters in the units involved numerous incidental characteristics on the bases of which relations may be established with other units having similar characteristics. The proliferation of possible relations follows an exponential curve as functions are increased arithmetically. A realization of the full potential number of relations, however, diminishes with size and complexity of the ecosystem. An understanding of that process requires recognition of another class of unit.

Complex Units

The discussion thus far has dealt mainly with simple functions, that is, the kind that can be carried on by individual human beings. Yet every individually performed function is usually joined with other functions to constitute a higher-order function carried on by a complex unit, that is, an organized group.[7] Complex units may be expected to take form whenever the conduct of a function exceeds the capabilities of a simple unit, an individual. That condition may arise where the variety of skills required is more than an individual can master, where a relatively large amount of capital is essential, and where the demand for the product is greater than a simple unit can supply. There are also transaction costs, to use the language of the economist (Williamson 1980). Complex units are formed, it is said, when transaction costs in a market context are greater than transaction costs in an integrated and centrally administered organization. Not only do such units reduce transaction costs, they act as proxies in the maintenance of many relations that lie beyond the individual's ability to manage. The complex unit produces economies of scale. The effects of complex-unit formation are not confined to a local context, for the absorption of transaction costs in a local market enables a unit to deal more effectively with transaction costs encountered in an extralocal market.

Although complex units appear in great variety in human ecosystems, they can be usefully sorted into two broad classes, namely, corporate and categoric units.

Corporate Units

An assemblage of simple units that are functionally differentiated and symbiotically integrated constitute an organic-like
or corporate unit. The corporate unit is the genus of many
species. Most primitive among such units are the family-
household and the village. The family-household operates as a
small division of labor engaged in a set of broadly defined
functions comprising the production and allocation of sustenance, the processing of materials and the fabrication of products, the training of the young, and the provision of services of
many kinds. The village is a looser division of labor founded
upon part-time family-household specialties. It raises the survival probabilities of the family-household to a higher power.

Improvements in the facility for mobility bring households
and villages within easier reach of one another. The potential
clienteles for the products of particular skills developed within
domestic units are widened thereby. Household specialization
is intensified. Some units concentrate larger shares of time and
energies on crafts, others may devote themselves to services,
while most may continue as food producers. The response to
opportunity for specialization is sometimes due to ineptitude
in competition for participation in a particular function. It
presupposes, however, the possession of an alternative capability of a kind that complements other functions.

The family-household has a number of disabilities as a unit
of specialized activity. Its methods of obtaining a labor supply,
that is, reproduction, gives no assurance that necessary skills
will be forthcoming. Marriage and kinship equivalents such as
adoption and apprenticeship are means of exercising a purposeful selectivity and thus of compensating for ineffectual
recruitment through reproduction. But the application of
rational criteria to personnel selection is always subject to
subversion by the persistence of prejudices bred in parochialism favoring kinship obligations. Moreover, since sentiment
cannot be extended effectively over great numbers, the family
can seldom attain or retain large size as a producing unit.
Hence the diversity of capabilities that can be represented in
its membership is limited. In fact, the variety of skills required
for many complex functions is apt to have a random occurrence so far as households are concerned. Small size also
restricts the amount of capital that can be assembled. The

family-household, then, for reasons of both restricted size and limited resources, is handicapped in the accumulation of technical lore and in the acquisition and use of elaborate tools.

The limitations inherent in the family-household, on the one hand, and the continuing thrust toward increasing specialization, on the other hand, lead to the formation of a new kind of unit. Historically, that appeared first as merely a rearrangement of simple skills in closer coordination. The factory, for example, was originally nothing more than a temporal and spatial regrouping of family-household functions. But it was soon discovered that the extrafamilial unit, of which the factory was the prototype, gave unlimited scope to the advance of specialization. It also provided a model that could be adapted to virtually all types of complex functions. Retail and service establishments, industrial corporations, government bureaus, schools of all kinds, hospitals, and charitable agencies are corporate units in the same sense, though they may differ in function, scale, and complexity. In historic perspective what was once a complex activity carried on by a relatively small, all-purpose kinship unit is transposed as a large number of simple functions variously linked in numerous highly specialized, complex units. As a general rule, the more frequent are the interactions among a set of functions, all of which are dependent on the environmental conditions mediated through a particular function, the greater is the probability that they will coalesce as a corporate unit.

The corporate unit embodies many of the features represented in the structure of the parent system. Hence it may properly be regarded as a subsystem. As in the parent system, the corporate unit has a key function, a function that transmits to member functions the effect of interactions with the systemic environment. Member functions are also ordered in sequences of transitive and connective relations. They differ, therefore, by degree of removal from direct contact with the key function as well as by type of specialization. Furthermore, the number of simple units in each function included in the corporate unit varies inversely with the cost of reproducing the skill of that function and directly with the number of simple units that utilize the product of that function. An important difference between system and subsystem remains, however. That is, while a parent system is moved toward openness to an ecumenic environment, its subsystems move toward closure.

The corporate unit acquires very specific membership criteria and a single point of contact with its system environment, the parent system.

Structural isomorphism, another expression of standardization, results from the necessity that all parts of an ecosystem maximize their intelligibility to one another. For otherwise exchanges and communication would be severely handicapped. Hence, all corporate units of a given size tend, in direct relation to the frequency of exchanges among them, to acquire counterpart functions and similar internal arrangements. The complements of officers, line and staff arrangements, accounting methods, and modes of governance approach a central tendency. The size assumption is necessary inasmuch as small units cannot encompass as much functional diversity as can larger ones. Consequently, small units collectively support specialized units that perform functions ordinarily included in the organizations of larger units, such as accounting, legal services, engineering, specialized maintenance, and others (cf. Brittain and Freeman 1980, 314). Scale economies for small units are realized in the system as a whole rather than in each unit.

Categoric Units

It will be recalled that interdependences develop also on the basis of similarities among the members of a population. Like units can pool their strengths in parallel or rhythmic actions and thereby raise their effectiveness far above the capabilities of individuals acting separately. Such a union, founded as it is on the commensal relationship, is the most rudimentary of human groupings. Yet it appears in ecosystems of all degrees of complexity and in almost unlimited variety. With advances in the scale and complexity of a system, categoric units, as commensalistic unions are called, multiply in number and become more formal in structure. The effect of system growth is to increase the difficulty of each individual unit's controlling the conditions essential to its functioning, for those conditions become so intermingled with other conditions and their connections removed through so many degrees of indirectness that they are not accessible to easy manipulation. The most available solution to the loss of power in simple units is coalescence with others of like kind to form categoric units. Therein lies the birth of political institutions.

Categoric units arise most commonly when an environmental relation is threatened. The threat may appear as an undifferentiated task too large for an individual to accomplish in a limited time, such as the harvesting of a crop before a damaging change in the weather. The threat may be a risk of losing land to an invader, a possible destruction of a road or other amenity in a residential area, or a technological shift that might render an occupation obsolete. If, however, the threat, having been disposed of, is not repeated, joint action ceases and the common characteristic recedes from attention. But some threats are recurrent and continuous. In that event the units affected will form a lasting association, which constitutes it a higher-order unit in the ecosystem.

The categoric unit is not confined to what can be described as vital interests. It is just as applicable to avocational interests of even the most inconsequential nature. There is virtually no interest or characteristic shared by two or more individuals that might not serve as the basis for a categoric unit. Homogeneity seems to be subdivisible without limit. In every instance the categoric association enables the members to accomplish more than they could achieve separately.

Another major impetus to categoric-unit formation stems from the nature of the simple units themselves. Units with similar characteristics make similar demands on their environment or on the system in which they are included. When the aggregate demand exceeds the supply of the material, the space, the customers, the employment opportunity, or whatever is the requirement, competition ensues. The greater the degree of likeness among units—the more they have in common—the greater the probability of competition among them when scarcities develop. The resulting contest, if uncontrolled, can be destructive, or at least costly. Thus like units sooner or later enter into collusive arrangements in order to limit, channel, or otherwise control the competitive relationship. In consequence, some units are excluded from access to the given resource space. Some, given an open system, may be able to cultivate latent abilities in a narrowing of specialization of one sort or another. But that also assumes a sufficient population in the system to provide an adequate clientele for the new function. If that condition is not present, the new specialty does not survive and the units involved may turn to simpler functions. They then may find themselves in competition with units at the lower functional level. Vertical mobility, either upward or downward, appears to be a possibility unique to the human ecosystem.[8] The alternative, which is shared with biotic ecosystems, is exclusion from the parent system through either migration or mortality.[9]

The establishment of a permanent categoric unit presupposes much more than a mere mass of parallel actions. When challenges are continuous or recurrent, mechanisms to secure and preserve cohesiveness must be developed. There must be means of summoning members to assembly, of gathering resources, of agreeing upon and administering rules, of devising programs of collective action, and so on. In short, some differentiation of function is essential to continuity. A symbiotic core emerges in the midst of an aggregate of like units. A religious sect, a labor union, a political party, for example, is composed of a mass of communicants and a small hierarchy of officials or specialists. With such an organization, the unit is able to pass beyond simple reactive behavior to positive or programmed action. It can then promote as well as protect the interests of its members.

In this respect the formalization of categoric units creates opportunities, within niches elsewhere in the system, for simple units eliminated from competition and at the same time augments the system's division of labor. Executive secretaries, educational directors, and clerical functionaries of various kinds are recruited from the same training programs upon which corporate units rely for comparable personnel. Furthermore, the articulation of categoric-unit programs with corporate-unit functions generates still other opportunities for specialization, as in arbitration, lobbying, and public relations.

The foregoing makes it apparent that categoric units are subject to the isomorphic tendencies operating throughout the system. They, too, must communicate with other units and submit to common operating conditions. Accordingly, and in the measure to which their interactions are frequent, they acquire similar complements of officers, employ uniform means of accounting for funds and properties, and govern themselves by parliamentary rules. They may even incorporate to gain the same legal protections and tax benefits enjoyed by corporate units.

The convergence of categoric and corporate units in some particulars does not eliminate important differences. One has to do with the criteria for membership. Individuals are admitted to corporate units on the strength of their abilities to perform specialized functions. Recruitment to the categoric unit rests on possession of the generic characteristics that define the unit—ethnic origin, religious belief, or occupational position. The manner of membership selection bears upon a difference in relation to the systemic environment. The corporate unit is adapted to serving a more or less anonymous clientele, that is, a market existing outside of its structure. In contrast, the categoric unit has no external clientele; its participants are all contained within the organization.[10] Hence the conditions that regulate the sizes of the two kinds of units are different.

Again, unlike the corporate unit in which size and complexity advance in close association, categoric-unit growth can develop large structural discontinuities. There can be and often are meteroric rises in numbers of members, with little or no concomitant increases in size of administrative hierarchies. Later, after membership increase may have subsided or ceased altogether, the corps of specialists may enter upon a phase of rapid increase as the unit becomes more fully involved in protecting and promoting the interests of its membership.

A Typology of Units

The corporate-categoric unit dichotomy lends itself to further refinement because the symbiotic and commensal relations find expressions in different settings, giving rise to a variety of units of each type. Of these the most primitive are manifested in different facets of the family. On the one hand, the family is a corporate unit, a division of labor in which children are nurtured, a sustenance enterprise is carried on, and many personal services are provided. On the other hand, members of a family household are at the same time enmeshed in a categoric unit represented by kinship linkages that function as a unit periodically in mutual aid arrangements.

More inclusive units occur on a territorial basis. In one perspective the village, the city, and the hierarchy of cities are corporate entities; they are symbiotic unions through which populations are able to occupy locations in space and time. In another perspective a territorially based corporate unit is also a categoric unit, that is, its members share a common interest in the maintenance of the facilities and institutions by which all live. They constitute a polity. There are also lesser units of territory whose occupants coact as categoric units, such as ethnic enclaves, neighborhoods, and ghettos.

A third basis on which complex units are constituted has no necessary familial or territorial reference. These, which have already been discussed at length, may be identified as associational in character. Examples of these and of the familial and territorial types of units are repeated in the following exhibit.

COMPLEX UNITS

Unifying Principle	Relational Structure	
	Corporate	*Categoric*
Familial	Household-producing and personal service unit	Kin, clan, and tribe
Territorial	Village, city, and ecumene	Polity, neighborhood, ethnic, enclave, ghetto
Associational	Industry, retail, store, school, government	Caste, class, sect, guild, club, union, professional organization

Power as a System Property

An ecosystem is, among other aspects, a power system. It is a mobilization of power to extract and control sustenance from its environment. Each function shares in that power to the extent that it contributes to system productivity. Inasmuch as functional contributions are unequal, system power is likewise unequally distributed. The mutually beneficial feature of symbiosis does not mean also equality of benefit. Power is disproportionally concentrated in the function that mediates critical environmental inputs to other functions, and they, in turn, possess system power in inverse relation to the number of functions intervening between each and the key function, given that productivity often eludes measurement. The organization of system power has its roots, as noted previously, in the environmental relationship and is manifested in the hierarchical ordering of functional specialization (Hawley 1963; Lincoln 1976).

Sooner or later the progress of specialization forces a subdivision of the key function. Increase in the diversity of materials and information utilized in an expanding system elaborates the environmental mediating function beyond the capacity of a single functional unit. Subdivision proceeds in two directions. On the one hand, the opening of additional and distinct avenues of contact with environment results in a sharing of the key function role with other units. What began as a monohierarchic system becomes multihierarchic. On the other hand, system complexity attaches technical tasks to the key function, tasks that demand skills of specially trained personnel. Accordingly, each key function comes to be served by a staff of experts. To the extent that the activity of a key function becomes contingent on a number of other functions, its share of system power is reduced, though it may retain a disproportionate share of the total. In fact, an effect of specialization at all levels is to decentralize power. But the centrifugal tendency has its limits, however. A delegation of responsibility of technical tasks enhances the importance of the coordinating function.

An important exercise of disproportionate power by units engaged in a key function is to accumulate capital with which to finance operating equipment, technical acquisitions, and system growth. The latter may or may not be an explicit objective of capital accumulation. But without a capital fund in one form or another, there can be no system growth. One does not need to be a neo-Marxist to agree that capital is built by withholding shares of net product from distribution to workers. Presumably the withholding of surplus product applies to

workers at all levels in the hierarchy. But the relative deprivation tends to be more severe at each lower level in the hierarchy. Moreover, the ostensible capital building process is subject to abuses. The resources set aside for the purpose may be
squandered in extravagant consumption on the part of the
custodians or in unwise applications.

It is in this connection that the categoric unit makes itself felt
as a political force. Having brought competition among its
members under control and having acquired an organization
that enables it to engage in positive action, the categoric unit is
in a position to redress some of the inequalities that derive
from the hierarchical power structure. Thus it enters into competition with key function units for shares of the net product.
Having achieved some success on that score, the categoric unit
may then enter into competition for generalized power in the
system, as, for example, in the determination of social policies.
But categoric-unit formation as an instrument of competition is
not confined to low-order functionaries. It is practiced at all
levels. Its effectiveness is further enhanced by pyramiding
categoric relations in federations of units. Worker unions
federate in regional association, and regional associations
combine to form national associations. White-collar and professional workers, as well as blue-collar workers, resort to the
same organizational strategy; social workers, doctors, law-
yers, actors, musicians, professors form local, regional, and
national categoric units to protect and promote their respective
interests. Nor are corporate units immune to the categoric-
union practice. Manufacturers of particular products, retailers, wholesalers, universities, and others enter into coaction
unions and thereby raise their powers to influence forces that
affect their welfares.[11] The categoric unit provides the organizational basis for conflict in an ecosystem; it is also the means
for the reduction of conflict.

The strength of a categoric unit as a competitive force is
normally confined to a specific interest or objective, and it
waxes and wanes with variations in the severity of the threat to
that common interest. Multiple memberships in different, in-
tersecting categoric units, some perhaps with conflicting interests, circumscribe the effective cohesiveness of any one
such unit. In the absence of crises, the one path to close
attachment of members to a given unit is through the joining of
other objectives to a specific one, that is, by generalizing the

relevance or value of a particular concern. The coincidence of two or more common interests among units in a complex system would seem to occur only under unusual circumstances, and the probability of its occurrence declines with size of membership in a category.

Number and Size of Complex Units

What has become known as population ecology is concerned with the carrying capacity of a system for number of complex units. It was observed in chapter 2 that the number of individuals engaged in the performance of functions is always smaller than the size of population, for the latter includes immature, superannuated, and disabled members. Moreover, since two or more individual functionaries are required to form a corporate unit and since each function is a full-time occupation, the number of corporate units must be fewer than the size of the working sector of the population. Whatever may be the maximum potential number of such units, that number tends to be further reduced by competition and the consequent appearance of fewer, larger-sized units. Number limitations such as these do not apply to categoric units. Their time-demands on members, though subject to considerable variations, are usually quite small, at least until a crisis arises. Thus each individual may be involved in two or more categoric units. The total number of categoric units doubtlessly varies with size of population and complexity of system structure. Costs of assembly and fees for support of unit programs impose restraints, however, on number per capita and on degree of active participation.

That there is a close relation between system complexity and population size has been shown in many studies. But the relationship does not always exhibit the same form. In simple systems the relation has been found to be exponential (Naroll 1956; Carniero 1967). On the other hand, where complexity is relatively far advanced, as in modern urban areas, the relation with size tends to be linear (Duncan 1957a; Ogburn and Duncan 1964; Winsborough 1960). The intercept of the linear slope, however, differs with the function of the city in relation to other cities (Galle 1963), and with the relative importance of transportation and communication industries (Clemente and

Sturgis 1978). In subsystems, on the other hand, the proportional size of the administrative personnel tends to decrease with size of unit (Anderson and Warkov 1961; Rushing 1967; Pondy 1969; Blau 1970; Mayhew et al. 1972; Mayhew and Levinger 1976). Consequently, size of administrative personnel is not a useful measure of complexity. The diverse research findings suggest that the way in which population is defined is of central importance. Kasarda (1974) examined selected aspects of the relationship at three levels of organization—corporate units, cities, and societies. He observed a direct relation between population size and the numbers of administrative, communication, and professional and technical personnel at all three levels. The managerial component of administration was found to vary inversely with size in corporate units, inconsistently with size in cities, and directly with size in societies.

Increase in system size and complexity creates conditions that foster, if not necessitate, increases in the sizes of subsystems. The ability of a subsystem to respond to the many relationships in which it is enmeshed by system complexity calls for special and often technical knowledge. Only in relatively large units can suitably qualified personnel be fully accommodated. Ability to serve a growing market, measured in part by size, affects the competitive power of a unit. In short, survival probabilities vary directly with size of unit (Aldrich and Auster 1986; Lincoln 1979). Size is the enemy of number. Although growth in size seems to blur unit boundaries, the boundary question is somewhat spurious. The vertical organization of an industry, for example, is an assemblage under a single administration of a number of formerly discrete units that may keep some external appearances of independence. But the merging usually involves an absorption of some of the smaller unit's processes by the larger unit, with the result that the appearance of separateness is illusory. The issue might be seen in clearer light in the case of a civil government. Although the government is composed of a number of bureaus and departments, no one of them is capable of separate existence.

Categoric units also find it expedient to grow to a size that enables them to operate on a scale comparable to that of the parent system. To fail to do so leaves the unit with a weak voice in policy matters that concern it. Nor can it, lacking size, accumulate the resources needed to provide a range of services to its members. That includes possession of the expertise needed for effective interaction with the many related units in a complex system. Hence the federation propensity mentioned earlier. McPherson (1983) reported that large voluntary, that is, categoric, organizations are more centrally located than are small units in an organization network and also have a more stable membership.

The principle of priority of external influences in change is just as apposite for subsystems as it is for a system. This is evident in the drift toward isomorphism with other units in the system. Each tends to model itself on the form prevailing and in direct relation to the frequency of interaction with other units. The reliance upon external influences is also manifested in the accumulation and utilization of information employed in a unit's internal processes. In a review of some two thousand case studies of technological innovations in business firms, Utterbach (1974) found that the information that proved critical to an innovation was usually imported from outside the firm. Exceptions could have been instances of concealed external influence due to poor reporting in what were in most cases ex post studies. A similar finding is reported by Baldridge and Burnham (1975) from their study of innovations in school systems, particularly in regard to reading programs and teaching techniques. Input from other organizations and the community at large were shown to be a major determinate in the design of a school system's procedures.

There remains the question of how the number of complex units, corporate units in particular, is regulated. One approach employs an adaptation of the biological evolutionary model described in a preceding chapter. Assuming a fixed carrying capacity in a system for units of each kind, and assuming further that units always tend to fill all available resource spaces, or niches, a system selects from a population of competing units those best fitted for each niche (Hannan and Freeman 1984). Environmental selection as used here is not to be regarded as contrary to my previously expressed view on selection. A new kind of unit does not differ in principle from any other randomly occurring element in an ecumenic environment. In this and in the more general case, the system is the selecting agent. In the birth of new industries, for example, the occupational and industrial diversity in the locality of birth has been shown to be an important environmental factor (Pennings 1982).[12]

Bidwell and Kasarda employ a modified evolution model in their explanation of the number of units comprising a system (1985, 208–9). In their view, number of units and the progress of complexity are determined by productivity. The long-run tendency is for productivity, and with it complexity, to either increase or decrease; no possibility is left for stability. This assumes a constantly perturbed environment and a limited ability in a system to compensate for environmental variations.

The selection principle has also been used to account for unit stability or inertia (Hannan and Freeman 1984). That is, units with high structural inertia have greater probabilities of selection by a systemic environment than have units with lesser degrees of structural inertia. This argument is advanced in opposition to adaptive potential as a basis for survival. But the relative importance of selection versus adaptive capacity would seem to depend on what is occurring in the parent system. If the system, or systemic environment, is constant over some span of time, the selection of subsystems with inert structures is most likely. On the other hand, where the system is growing and becoming more complex, subsystem survival would seem to require a large measure of adaptive capacity. To argue that structural continuity in subsystems is the guarantor of adaptive capacity is to make the distinction between selection and adaptation somewhat meaningless.

Unit fitness for a niche poses both conceptual and measurement problems. If fitness is represented by survival, the concept wears the appearance of circularity. Similarly with the measurement of resource space or niche width. These risks can be avoided by treating the matters entirely in probabilistic terms. Thus the question is: Given stated conditions, what is the probability that units of a certain kind will survive, that is, will be selected? An event that can raise the probability in specific cases is the appearance of an altogether new niche resulting from a technological breakthrough (Brittain and Freeman 1980, 321). But that does not entirely eliminate the risk of circularity. A more solid footing for a probabilistic approach lies with system size. The greater the size, the greater the probable support for units with higher degrees of specialization. Other pertinent conditions are rate or volume of intersystem communications, scope of a market, and amount of stability in intersystem relations.

In eliminating some number of units from claims on a resource space, competition allows other units to attain greater size, subject to the amount of resource space available. Again, some units, "specialist" units for example, may be absorbed as subunits of "generalist" units, to use the terms of Hannan and Freeman. That occurs when, as noted previously, transaction costs among separate units prove higher than are such costs within an inclusive unit. The amount of a particular function carried on in a system probably remains constant, ceteris paribus, whether the number of units performing that function is many or few. But where there are economies of scale, the costs of providing a given quantity of a function should decline as a few large units replace many smaller ones.

Subsystem Networks

Symbiotic modes of relationship develop among complex as well as among simple units (cf. Laumann, Galaskiewicz, and Marsden, 1978, 461). Unit specialization necessitates interunit exchanges and dependence. While that applies to all parts of a system, particularly close interdependences lie in various combinations of selected corporate and categoric units. Consequently an ecosystem may be viewed as a set of networks. Thus Craven and Wellman (1973) speak of the "network city."

Networks form around both producing and service classes of functions. A producing network may include not only a basic manufacturing unit and its suppliers, but also advertisers, retailers, maintenance services, labor unions, and technical schools. Most such networks exist as loosely bounded interaction fields. But high communication costs support a tendency toward a coalescence of some parts of the network into a single organization. Network involvement, however, is also the source of scale economies that would not otherwise be available to small units (Lincoln 1979).

Service networks are of many kinds. Prominent among them is that concerned with the physical structure of a city. That network may include land subdividers, realtors, building contractors, building material suppliers, construction workers' unions, inspectors' offices, and planning commissions. A welfare network embraces social agencies, united funds, social worker associations, service clubs, courts, and churches. Hospitals, doctors' and dentists' offices, pharmacies, pharmaceutical manufacturers, testing laboratories, medical schools, and professional associations form a health service network. Although policies in such areas may be written in legislative halls, the frequent interactions among the units involved in each instance produce an accumulation of understandings, agreements, and practices that shape the interpretations of official policies.

The structures of production networks tend toward a clearer hierarchical form than that which characterizes service networks, for in the former the interunit relations are usually aserial, that is, units are not interchangeable in their transitive relationship. Even so, however, their structures are loose, due largely to the participation of some member units in two or more networks. Financial agencies, transportation and communication services, and government regulatory bureaus are active in virtually all networks in a system. Greater fluidity prevails in service networks, since transitivity there is seldom accompanied by aseriality of relations. The one common structural property in all kinds of networks is a key unit that is instrumental in generating the flow of resources into the network (Benson 1975; Galaskiewicz 1979). Still the looseness of network structure imposes restraints on the power of the key unit. In competing for shares of the system's resources, the network must contend with the several categoric units to which its member units belong. That is another source of friction in system change.

Structural Rigidities

Structural inertia, though it may have survival value for a subsystem within a system, or for a system among interacting systems, can be carried to the point of loss of responsiveness to environmental shifts. Given a system exposed to an ecumenic environment, such as is the focus of attention throughout this discussion, excessive inertia is apt to afflict the parts rather than the whole. The condition is often transitory, however.

The failure of a subsystem to change at the rate its complementary subsystems are changing may be true at one moment in time but may be overcome at a later moment. Change moves unevenly through a system. A lag can result from various circumstances, such as faults in the communication linkages with sources of information, insufficient capital with which to modify procedures, or a lack of qualified personnel.

Where rigidity threatens to become a lasting state, it has its roots for the most part in overcentralization. That shows itself in either of two ways. It may appear in situations where most if not all decisions are referred to a key functionary. In the absence of delegation of authority, the number of subordinates reporting to an administrator affects his ability to respond promptly. Where the number is large, the result may be loss of time and stagnation of activity. Or the stagnation may be one in which, as Weber observed (1922, 650–78), there is an overspecification of rules and criteria for action by each of the several functions in the system. The resulting loss of flexibility tends to isolate the afflicted subsystem from the parent system.

Mention was made earlier of the tendency toward closure in corporate subsystems. That may be most prominent in large units where size has allowed them to include in their organizations many of the services their production processes require. Any movement toward closure invites loss of environmental responsiveness. That may take the form of a subordination of a unit's initial function to ancillary or even nonproductive functions. Survival calls for a balance between closure in some particulars and an openness to vital information sources.

Convergence in Changing Systems

I have thus far dealt with ecosystem development in an abstract fashion. In doing so I have passed over much diversity among systems of different times and places. A reasonable question concerns the rationale for generalization without a presentation of data on the many kinds of individual cases. But since the task of historic-comparative analyses has been performed a number of times by competent scholars (e.g., Goldschmidt 1959; Lenski and Lenski 1982), in the interest of economy I will move on to a theoretical approach to the question. Foregoing discussions have laid a foundation for such an approach.

A principle stated earlier for subsystems may be extended to systems as wholes on the assumption that under certain conditions small and large organizations are subject to similar organizing forces and restraints. What has been called the principle of isomorphism holds that system structures converge upon a common form to the extent that their interactions are frequent. Although the various ecosystems of humanity were formed in widely different circumstances and have in each instance been exposed to different historical experiences, the ecosystems have tended to become more alike as their interactions have increased because communication requires a standardization of terms of reference, operating procedures, and forms of organization. Thus modes of organizing industrial, distributing, and financial industries, patterns of occupational composition, the apparatus of government including departmental specialization, courts, customs and visa controls, planning agencies, and other regulatory arrangements, types of educational institutions and programs, and medical services all gravitate toward a mean. That this is true has been demonstrated quantitatively several times over (Meyer, Boli-Bennett, and Chase-Dunn 1975; Karsh and Cole 1968). The process may be delayed by the predilections of totalitarian governments, but it can be contravened only by isolation from communication networks.[13]

The convergence hypothesis is not without its critics (Weinberg 1969; Moore 1979; Skinner 1976; Bendix 1964, 5–15). Criticisms have claimed an unwarranted acceptance of evolution theory, an exaggeration of the effects of interdependence among systems, and a technological determinism. Most critics rest their cases upon indications that convergence has nowhere been complete, that many uniquenesses are to be found. But it is no contradiction of the hypothesis to find that, even after extended periods of intersystem exchanges, differences remain. For that matter, varieties of traditions and beliefs, of speech patterns, of legal arrangements and political processes, for example, are found within systems with long histories of internal structural integration. Convergence should be regarded as a process rather than as a consummation.[14]

How profoundly the effects of convergence may be expected to penetrate the organization of interacting systems is a question that has not been fully addressed. The answer will doubtless depend on the rate of increase in frequency of interaction. It will be affected, too, by the rate of change in degree of equality of access to information flows prevailing within the populations of related systems. But that equality in that regard will ever be complete is unlikely.

In sum, the position argued in these pages is that all systems are subject to similar principles of organization in the measure to which they possess corresponding efficiencies in transportation and communication. That limiting condition determines size of population, scope of territorial access, and opportunity for participation in information flows.

Propositional Résumé

Assumptions

2-H2, 2-H3 Hierarchy in system structure results from the interaction of population with environment.

3-H3 Cumulative change presupposes increases in accessible area and in population.

4-A1 Population increases to the size defined by the staff requirements of the system.

4-A2 Specialization advances to a maximum permitted by mobility costs.

Hypotheses

4-H1 Specialization of function begins whenever the number of units utilizing a service or a product becomes large enough to support the full-time conduct of the given activity.

4-H2 Specialization varies intensively and extensively inversely with mobility costs.

4-H2.1 Increases in intensity of specialization of any given function are accompanied by increases in intensity of specialization of all complementary functions.

4-H3   Specialization of function(s) and standardization of terms and conditions of operation vary together.

4-H4   As specializations increase arithmetically, the potential number of relations increases geometrically.

4-H5   The amount of time allocated to mobility varies directly with the number of relations among functions.

4-H6   The greater the extent to which functions are subject to the conditions mediated by a particular function, the greater is the probability that they will combine to constitute a complex unit (a subsystem).

4-H6.1   Combination in a complex unit reduces the transaction costs among combined functions, that is, congestion costs due to exponential increase in relations.

4-H7   Complex units develop on each of two axes: (*a*) on the basis of complementary differences (corporate units), and (*b*) on the basis of common environmental requirements (categoric units).

4-H8   Corporate units tend to replicate the structural properties of the parent ecosystem.

4-H9   Corporate units tend toward closure regardless of the openness of the ecosystem.

4-H10   Categoric units form among units that make similar demands on environment whenever the probability of realizing such demands is threatened.

4-H10.1 Competition, arising whenever demand exceeds supply, is a source of categoric-unit formation.

4-H10.2 Categoric-unit formation tends to equalize power distribution among functions in a hierarchy.

4-H11   Categoric units acquire symbiotic cores (administrative structure) as they gain permanence.

4-H12   Structural isomorphism advances among complex units with increases in the frequency of their interactions.

4-H13   Complex-unit sizes vary systematically with size of ecosystem.

4-H13.1 Relation of size of membership to complexity of structure differs as between corporate and categoric units, that is, the clientele of the one is external to the unit, while the clientele of the other is internal to the unit.

4-H14 Principles of organization apply across all levels of ecosystem scale.

5

Cumulative Change:

Expansion in

Time and Space

An ecosystem, obviously enough, is a finite entity; it exists in time and space. The two dimensions measure, at least as a first approximation, the scale of the system. They also measure the ways in which the parts of the system are arrayed relative to one another. All ecosystems exhibit temporal and spatial patterns. Scale and pattern change with accumulation, for what is accumulated crowds the available time and space and must be re-sorted into workable configurations.

The high visibility of the spatial dimension, however, is apt to conceal the temporal dimension of a system. That this has not always been so is attested by the origins of many spatial measures in the time consumed in movements of various kinds.[1] Nevertheless, spatial measures have come to be used as surrogates for temporal measures. Interdependence assumes mutual accessibility of the units concerned, and accessibility is measured by the time spent in coming into contact. The necessary recurrence of interdependent relationships imparts to them a rhythmic character. With increases in number and variety of interdependence, the many rhythms must be scheduled and coordinated. This is accomplished in the elaboration of an ecosystem. By that means, order is imposed on the uses of space. The order is a distributional pattern expressive of the time costs of recurrent movements in a system.

A Generalized Space-Time Model

Broadly considered, a temporal-spatial pattern represents a resolution of opposing tendencies. On the one hand, interdependence with its demands for interunit accessibility exercises a centripetal tendency; units of organization are drawn toward a concentration of locations. Human settlement is characteristically nucleated therefore. On the other hand, competition for location, operating in conjunction with diverse location requirements, develops a centrifugal tendency. Units are thrust outward from a point of maximum accessibility in keeping with their inabilities to use space intensively. Thus the general outline of a system's pattern includes an inner core and an outer periphery with a graded, though not necessarily monotonic, decline of density of occupance from core to periphery. Both the slope and extent of the gradient are variable, depending on the composition of mobility costs.

Accordingly, in any given state of local transportation technology, there tends to be an optimum density of concentration, a density that is most conducive to the efficient functioning of the system. Too low a density makes for relatively high costs of conducting exchanges of all kinds and allows destabilizing influences to enter a system. Conversely, too great a density raises costs through time lost in congestion and related frictions, introducing different destabilizing forces.

As a general principle it may be stated that in any given state of technology the costs of movement, that is, the time and energy consumed in movement, vary with density in a U-shaped pattern. That is, costs increase more than proportionally with density variations in each direction from an optimum point.

It is useful to recognize that the territory within which a human ecosystem operates manifests three different scales that, for want of better terms, may be designated local, sometimes referred to as communal, regional, and interregional. The local scale, delineated usually by the distance that can be traveled in an hour's time, encompasses the manifold interactions that occur with a daily periodicity. A regional scope is bounded by exchange relations involving a particular center which occur with a lesser periodicity, weekly or fortnightly, and are therefore restricted in number and kind. The third, or interregional territory, is an ill-defined area lying beyond regional boundaries and in which a few selected points are the foci of even more specific relations with the given center. The dimensions of the three areas are temporal as well as linear.

Another feature of the territorial aspect of all but the most primitive systems is their multinucleated character, unlike the models proposed by von Thunen (1966) for a region and later by Burgess (1925) for a communal area. The several centers are disposed about a transport route network, however crude it may be. Although in the crude transport state the several centers may be relatively undifferentiated, their locations in the network differ with respect to the access they provide for center-to-center interrelations and for relations to a larger universe.

Location proves critical in the initiation of an expansion process. The strategic site is possessed by the center with the easiest access to both regional and interregional influences. It is there that the requisite information for improvements in transportation and communication technologies has the greatest probability of accumulating. But because the technologies for long- and short-distance movements tend to occur unevenly, territorial expansion advances first on one scale and then on another. A prior development of long-distance relative to short-distance transportation issues from a combination of organizational, technical, and historical circumstances. The accumulation of information at a strategically located site and its transformation to more elaborate techniques and division of labor call for increase in the variety and amounts of raw materials. Since the various materials are found at different locations, it is necessary to assemble them at a single location for processing and fabricating. But the technical means for transporting materials in bulk, for example, the seagoing vessel and the railway, are ill suited for the short haul because their large capital requirements favor a distribution of operating and amortization costs over the long haul.[2] Finally, it seems that technological advances generally appear first in large and cumbersome form before reduction to smaller, more refined forms. It should not be surprising then to find improvements in the facilities for short-distance or local movement following some time after advances in long-distance transport techniques. But the delay, though long in one phase of expansion, need not remain so in all later expansion phases.

At the risk of elevating a historical fact to a general principle, let us accept the priority of improvements in long-distance transportation and communication. Regardless of the mix of factors that may enter into an explanation of that disparity, the outcomes bear certain similarities in all but a few instances.

Interregional Expansion

Historically the territorial reach of an ecosystem occurred first in an extension of relations over great distance without corresponding enlargements of either the scope of the community center from which the relations originated or the scope of its regional influence. That rested on the relatively easy movement of bulk goods over riverine and coastal water courses and the use of pack animals for the overland carriage of exotic and high-value commodities.[3] The early interregional linkages were feeble and tenuous, to be sure, and they were probably more important for the information transmitted than for the goods carried. Even so, an extension of relations beyond regional boundaries presupposes a fairly close integration of differentiated activities at a core, that is, within a communal area. The composition of functions in that local organization depends somewhat on how the expansion is effected. Where expansion is pursued through military means, organizational development at the center is led chiefly by an elaboration of administrative mechanisms. The management of conquered territories and the exploitation of their resources calls for cadres of managers, record keepers, messengers. But where distant relations are founded primarily on trade, with little or no exercise of military power, organizational change occurs mainly in the commercial sector; it issues in the rise of banking agencies, wholesalers and middle men, various craftsmen, and transportation experts. One way or another, large urban centers flourish at the centers of webs of interregional relations. But they grow in density of organization and population with no corresponding enlargement of space, apart from the additions at their peripheries of cell-like appendages, lending the aspect of a polyp to each such agglomeration.

Further advances, particularly in navigation and ship design, provide additional impetus to the establishment of long-distance relations. An effect is to favor the growth of centers at the margins of regions while inland towns and districts stagnate and decline (Phythian-Adams 1978; Mantoux 1927, 117). Yet the risks of water travel often neutralize its cost advantages (Braudel 1966, 276–85). A countereffect is a stimulation of efforts to find ways of improving overland transportation.[4]

That an extension of interregional linkages precedes regional integration relative to an organized core is not just a historical accident as indicated by modern repetitions of the phenomenon. Many new nations have cultivated their extraterritorial trade and diplomatic relations while allowing their metropolitan hinterlands to languish in relative isolation and neglect. To argue that the practice is a heritage of a colonial experience does not account adequately for its continuation in a postcolonial period. Interregional exchanges seem to provide the simplest stimulus to the maturation of organization at a center that can then be effectively extended over a surrounding territory.

Regional Expansion

Alfred Weber (Friedrich 1929) and C. H. Cooley (1930) were among the first to recognize the effect of a route intersection on the accumulation of industries and services to constitute a city. A more general significance attaches to such sites, however. There strangers meet and exchange information and ideas as well as goods, and it is there, consequently, that inventions occur most frequently. The role of the settlement at a transportation node, that is, a city, in technical and cultural change has been shown in numerous studies (Redfield and Singer 1954; Turner 1940; Thompson 1962; Pred 1966, 86ff.; Feller 1971; Higgs 1975).[5] There thus develops an organization capable of extending its influence over a surrounding region.[6]

An intensification and integration of intraregional relations had to await the development of overland transportation. While there were many early beginnings, the most active period of road construction took place after the formation of centralized governments. Extralocal powers are needed for the preemption of lands, the levying of taxes, the provision of inducements to innovation, and the policing of thoroughfares. As road networks were nearing completion, the steam railway made its appearance and within a few decades solidified patterns of regional organization. The unfolding of a rail network followed a sequence that had characterized the earlier development of highway networks. It began with radial routes fanning out from a point where interregional and intraregional routes converge. Later branches off the radial routes linked interstitial settlements to the central node. Finally, lateral lines were built to tie radial and branch lines into a web of interconnections.[7] At each step in the unfolding route network, the accessibility values of localities are altered.

There follows a redistribution of functions and population, leading to differential growth at nodal points, varying in correspondence with the degree of access possessed. Communities that are bypassed by the improved means of travel wither and disappear, their functions absorbed by more favorably located communities. Those at minor nodal points survive as local service centers and raw material transshipment points. Others with superior transport locations grow in size or the strength of a greater number and variety of functions. The largest size and the greatest functional diversity are attained at the point of maximum accessibility. Overall functional redistribution is accompanied by functional obsolescence and replacement. Handicraft industries are displaced by mechanized industries, generalists succumb to specialists, formerly discrete functions are gathered into complex units, and intermediary functions multiply to provide the linkages in transitive sequences.

The effects of the development of medium- and long-distance routes on the reorganization of activities in a region, however, are lumpy. Rail lines and road surfaces not only smooth the way for vehicular use, they also channel movements in specific lanes. Accordingly, the benefits of cost reductions are distributed unevenly over the region. In the case of the railway, interstitial areas of more than twenty miles distance—the team-haul distance—on either side of a rail line were left in their pristine isolation. Moreover, although system expansion is responsible for the development of a route network, once established the network guides and allocates subsequent system growth until new transportation forms appear. It then becomes possible to absorb into a system the bypassed interstitial zones.

Differential growth produces a more or less symmetrical size-of-place and diversity-of-function hierarchy in a region. Where industry is organized on a handicraft basis, there tends to be a spatial symmetry to the hierarchy. But the spatial symmetry disappears with the mechanization of industry and the growing importance of interregional relations (Mark and Schwirian 1967). Hierarchy remains, but is cast in functional terms primarily. A correlation of size of place with specialization of functions performed has been demonstrated (Duncan and Reiss 1956; Duncan et al. 1960). As noted previously, specialization presupposes enough users of the produce to permit a full-time pursuit of the activity. In more general terms, size is related to position on a dominance scale. The largest place, by virtue of its strategic location, occupies a dominant position in its region. In having the principal and most direct contact with an interregional universe, it sets the conditions under which the various subdominant communities operate.[8] Its influence is transmitted downward and outward over the region through the size-of-place chain. Thus a dominant center functions in the same way in a regional system that a key function does in a corporate unit.

The functional position of a subcenter in the territorial division of labor embraced in a size-of-place hierarchy usually has a characteristic demographic composition associated with it. Each industrial-occupational mix is selective of types of people, with reference to age, sex, education, and family composition (Kass 1977). The demographic differentiation of resident populations is more pronounced within near distances of dominant centers. Subcenters in those zones tend toward specialization as industrial, residential, or service functions (Schnore 1957, 1963). Type of specialization is accompanied by differences in levels of personal income and other fiscal characteristics (Lincoln and Friedland 1976; Logan 1976). Socioeconomic strata acquire a territorial distribution.

The boundary of a regional system may be said to lie on an isoline plotted on the points at which the value of goods and services produced for exchange with or through the dominant center approximate the costs of transporting them from the periphery to the center. Such a boundary is unstable inasmuch as production and other costs vary from time to time. Nor does a dominant center have exclusive control over its region. Adjacent systems penetrate the territories of one another by virtue of various unique specializations (Pappenfort 1959).

Center Expansion

In the course of system expansion resulting from improvements in long-distance transportation, with short-distance transport technology constant, for example, in an animal-powered regime, the scope of the local or communal system, whether dominant or subdominant, remains unchanged. This being the case, the redistributions that build a territorial division of labor produce increasing concentrations of units and functions within a more or less fixed amount of space. Concentration is imperative as long as a primitive state of communication technology preserves a closely limited territorial span of administrative control. Concentration of units and centralization of control are coincident in the spatial organization. Railway organization, because of the spatial spread of its operations, was a notable exception (Chandler 1977, 87–94), an exception that would not have been possible without cheap long-distance communication via the telegraph. Confined though the scope of a local organization may prove to be, that organization serves as the engine that drives the process of regional development. It supplies the technical personnel, the raw-material processing units, the administrative apparatus, and the gateway to extra regional markets, all of which are essential to a regional division of labor.

Centripetal tendencies produce different distributional patterns within communal space, depending on the prevailing costs of short-distance or intramural mobility, the extent of extrafamilial corporate organization, and the size of agglomeration. Holding mobility costs constant at a high level and assuming relatively slight organization in extrafamilial units, the degree of agglomeration cannot be large. The spatial pattern will then show a distribution of residents in which socioeconomic status varies inversely with distance from the principal interest center in the local area. For most of the resident population, the interest center has its prime importance for avocational and ceremonial rather than for commercial uses. Affluence determines the ability to enjoy proximity to the center. Sjoberg (1960) has shown such a pattern to be characteristic of the preindustrial city. But should size of agglomeration follow a trend of increase despite primitive and therefore high costs of local mobility, a growth of extrafamilial organization necessitates a close coincidence of residence and workplace. The increasing pressure of density on mobility costs breaks up a mono-centered pattern with its inverse correlation of social-economic status and distance. In its stead a cellular pattern appears. Workers' residences are located around workplaces, and workers draw their respective religious, recreational, and other services to their work-residence enclaves.[9] The several cells are linked in a loose unity by a few thin lines of dependence on a principal transportation node at which units providing political and various exotic services are located.

Although lagging in development, technological change ultimately affects the efficiency of short-distance, intracommunal movement. First the street railway, then the telephone and later the motor vehicle raised the scope of the sixty-minute radius from three to over twenty miles. A separation of homes from workplaces begins and progresses quicker and farther among residents who can afford the costs of daily commuting trips. At the same time a closer temporal integration of functional units becomes feasible; it finds expression in a new spatial pattern. The old cellular pattern gives way to a concentration of an increasing number of functions at or near the point of intersection of intramural and extramural lines of transportation and communication. A competition for sites at the point of intersection results in a spread of units, which corresponds to a direct relation of distance removed from the point and inability, for reasons of costs or functional requirements, to use space intensively. The intensity-of-use gradient is interrupted at points where lateral and radial intramural routes intersect. At such points competition for sites is repeated at a lower level of intensity, giving rise to short and steep intensity-of-use gradients. Thus in large agglomerations, primary, secondary, and even tertiary interest centers appear in a web of radial and lateral routes. The pattern, in other words, exhibits a multinucleated form (cf. Berry 1965).

Since area increases as the square of distance from a point, the distribution by intensity of use proves also to be a distribution by density of occupance. The distribution conforms more or less closely to a gradient of decreasing density, the highest value falling at the point of maximum accessibility and the lowest value at a point from which it is not practicable to move daily to and from the point of peak density.[10] Thus another isoline can be identified from traffic flows. That line lies where the costs of daily travel to a center exceed the savings in site rents that can be realized in a more distant location. But accessibility may not always be greatest at the point of intersection of intramural and extramural transportation routes. For great densities produce congestion costs that detract from the accessibility values of such locations. Usually when that occurs the node of intramural routes shifts away from the node of extramural routes and toward the geometric center of population.

The redistribution of units incidental to a relaxation of restraints on short-distance movements is manifested also in different spatial groupings. The earlier mixed clusters of residences, retail stores, and leisure-time service units around employing units give way to a separation of unlike activities and their relocation in relatively homogeneous enclaves. Not only is there a gross segregation of manufacturing, retailing, and residential uses of space, the process moves to a finer-grained compartmentalization, especially among population types. Areas of ethnic, racial, income, and family homogeneity appear. The tendency is for units with similar environmental requirements to congregate in space. The similarity of requirement may be of many kinds, differing with type of unit, such as low land or rental costs, proximity to transport installations and other external economies, easy access to religious, educational, or other services, and suitability for family needs. This tendency underlies and simplifies the application of invidious segregation policies through such means as protective covenants, subdivision controls, zoning ordinances. Enclaves of that kind, however, may break up as the homogenizing effect of race, ethnicity, or poverty is weakened by the onset of socioeconomic differentiation within the respective categories.

Intensity of use of space is measured in large part by the tempo of activity in that space, as represented, for example, by the number of communications and transactions per interval of time or the rate of turnover of inventories. Since frequency of activity is affected by the number of specialized units, tempos increase with size of agglomeration.[11] Size also influences the distribution of functions through a time space. While the alternation of activity and rest periods sets the basic rhythm in an organized population, growth in size increases also the probability that enough people will be available to support some functions during off-hours. It becomes possible, therefore, for a system to expand in time with no corresponding enlargement of space. As the activities of units, first leisure-time units, later producing units with multishift work schedules, invade off-hour periods, the tempo of a system becomes arhythmic (Hawley 1950, chap. 15; Melbin 1978).

Deconcentration versus Centralization

The resorting of residences to create a direct association of socioeconomic status with distance from a central core may be viewed as the beginnings of deconcentration of the components of a communal system. The facilitation of vehicular travel permits units to locate farther apart without loss of contact. But also the extension of hard-surfaced street networks into adjoining territory, the lengthening of water, sewer, and power lines, and the spread of various other urban-type services enable population and other units to seek the more abundant and cheaper lands on the moving periphery of an expanding community.

The centrifugal drift is led by units that are least encumbered by large space requirements. That has usually been new cohorts of families and small-scale personal service establishments. Industrial units are held in place for a time by the greater, though dwindling, benefits of agglomeration over congestion costs (Segal 1976). Eventually the technological changes calling for new building designs and increased amounts of space, coupled with a widening availability of services to industry, lead industries to follow in the centrifugal drift. An inertia embodied in the physical structures accumulated in the concentration phase makes the outward movement somewhat sluggish. Old cities, for example, have retained some of their pattern features well into the period of declining short-distance mobility costs (Guest 1969; Hunter 1971; Haggerty 1971; Hawkes 1973). Units least affected by the

deconcentration tendencies are those specialized in administration.

Not only does the land scale of organization grow larger, it
becomes more involuted. That is, the multinucleated form is
carried into the zone of expansion, that is, suburban area, and
is there accentuated. The regrouping of population and of
industries and service units in numerous and for the most part
smaller nuclei produces a new pattern in the geometry of
urban settlement. Manifold results follow. While the revenue
base of the older core area is eroded, the multiplication of
governmental units increases the total government overhead.
Administrative autonomy in each suburban unit, combined
with their differentiation as to type of resident and type of
economic base, allows for great unevenness in the number and
quality of services available to residents. Traffic flows become
increasingly lateral and circumferential, in contrast to the
radial movements that formerly prevailed. A dispersion of
destinations, vocational and avocational, together with the
continuing removal of personal services from households to
extrahousehold units, increases the number of vehicular trips
and the average mileage traveled per person per day. Efficiency gains through the general lowering of residential densities are counteracted somewhat by increases in traffic
densities.[12] Longer-distance moves, on the other hand, have
the effect of reducing commuting distances for the movers
(Morrison and Abrahamse 1982). In other words, commuting
movements—the daily recurring movements of a population—increase at the expense of residence changes.

The spread of daily travel destinations within local areas,
constituting what one observer has called a "community without propinquity" (Webber 1963), seems paradoxical. For it is
associated with a continuing tendency toward residential
clustering in homogeneous socioeconomic enclaves. The phenomenon is most pronounced in the middle and upper
socioeconomic levels. Evidently in those categories the residential locale represents a neighborhood of "limited liability,"
to use Janowitz's term (1952, 222–25). Segregation of residents
by type enables them to protect specific common interests, for
example, property values, with a minimum of involvement in
the affairs of coresidents.

Deconcentration is not confined to the enlargement of local

areas. It leaps the boundaries of those areas and reaches far
into surrounding regions and beyond. The rise of new loca-
tion-free industries, the rapid growth of service industries,
and the labor-displacing mechanizations of old, heavy industries radically alter the territorial distribution of job opportunities. Government entitlement programs to retirees and welfare
clients allow them to relocate their residences at will. Consequently large urban agglomerations give way to many smaller
ones in what constitutes a general regrouping of the urban
population.

As the pace of technological change shifts from transportation to communication, however, the major centers retain
some elements of their roles in an interregional ecosystem.
Instantaneous point-to-point communications, while facilitating deconcentration, foster an increasing centralization of control. The two processes are separated and move in opposite
directions. By way of illustration, in the United States the
properties of production facilities controlled from central
offices located outside a region increased between 1955 and
1975 in all but one of nine regions and by over 35 percent in
southern and western regions (Ross 1982). Centralization of
control appears with growth in scale of unit size. That may
come about through an absolute growth in response to
penetration of more extensive markets, from the creation of
branches in outlying locations, or from the merging of scattered stores and plants under a single management. A similar
trend is found among categoric units as local units enter into
district and regional federations with central offices in strategic
centers. The movements toward centralization, corporate and
categoric, lay a more elaborate structure of relationships upon
a size-of-place hierarchy.

Offices controlling multiunit subsystems congregate at
principal communication nodes because their functions place
a premium on direct and quick access to information flows.
Clustering also enables them to collectively support a number
of services to administration, such as financing, marketing,
advertising, printing, and various technical advisory services.
And, since administrative functions are among the last to be
standardized and the last to be removed from the barter
economy, they rely to a large extent on face-to-face negotia-
tions and exchanges.

But as further advances in communication technology accumulate, the advantages of dominant centers as locations for central office functions diminish. It becomes possible to locate such functions at any of many alternative sites, some at great distances from dominant centers. That option is supported also by the deconcentration of external economies; standardization of their processes and low-cost communications relieve them of the necessity for close proximity to clienteles (Hoover and Vernon 1959, 49–53). How far the dispersion of central office functions can be carried will depend on what, if any, benefits remain in a close clustering of their locations.

Communication advances also reduce the need for daily travel in pursuit of a growing number of personal services and interests. Just as the telephone eliminated the messenger, the radio and television have threatened the survival of conventional entertainment services. Access to news and information, to religious services, to political argumentation, as well as to entertainment, may be had merely by pressing a button and adjusting a television dial. Computerized transmission of monies minimizes the number of trips to banks and to many markets.

The gap between long- and short-distance transportation costs continues to be narrowed. The piggybacking of truck trailers on railway flatcars, the close linking of air freight and local truck delivery, and the use of container ocean shipping have merged the advantages of long- and short-haul facilities. The telephone, used initially for short-distance communications, has undergone repeated improvements in transmission techniques that have extended flat-rate zones around cities and cheapened long-distance uses. Transmission of radio and television communications via satellite is now instantaneous over maximum distances. Accordingly, site values tend to become homogenized over regional and interregional areas. Deconcentration moves in fairly close association with reductions in mobility costs. In more general terms, decreasing mobility costs convert small, simple, and territorially localized systems to large, complex, and territorially extensive systems.

In closing this section, one important question remains to be considered: How typical is the described sequence of changes in the spatial pattern of organization within local and regional areas? Is it probable that the phenomenon of convergence repeats in its late phases a given series of changes of pattern? An implication of the argument developed in these pages suggests an answer in the affirmative. In other words, to the extent that different systems repeat a given history of changes in transportation and communication technology, they will also repeat a series of spatial patterns. Furthermore, since spatial patterns are expressive of organizational patterns, the latter will also change in accordance with changes in transportation and communication. Granted, this assertion is something of a petitio principii. Nevertheless, its importance warrants its statement.

Ecosystem and Polity

It is desirable at this point to take up the matter of boundaries in a more direct fashion. The preceding discussion has touched upon boundaries of both qualitative kinds, but without explicit attention to their characteristics. In turning to that now, I risk belaboring the obvious in order to put the matter in an ecological context. Let me begin with some elementary considerations.

For a habitat to be made livable, a localized population must arrive at consensus on the pooling of resources for providing streets, market and meeting places, water and sewer service, protective services, and other common utilities. Out of such a categorical response to habitat needs, a local population emerges as a polity. As a polity it is able to mobilize the power required for provision of utilities and for deciding how much area is to be served by the utilities. The local population in its capacity as a polity draws a boundary around itself. The boundary approximates initially the scope of the daily activities of the members of the population. It does not, however, embrace the total area over which the vital interests of that population are spread. The mere dynamics of shifting and changing functional relations seem always to keep a system's scope well beyond that of a polity. Thus there are two kinds of boundaries—one political, the other systemic. The one is explicit, circumscribed, and fairly static, though subject to ordinance; the other is implicit in functional relations, extensive, variable, and elusive to observation.

How the centrifugal drift of the units of a local organization affects the political administrative organization of the locality is determined in large part by the degree to which local government autonomy is centralized or decentralized. Where it is decentralized such that many minor civil divisions possess degrees of autonomy, a deconcentrating community may encounter strong resistance to an extension of its boundaries to keep pace with the outward movement of its components. The residents of contiguous civil divisions tend to unite in categorical responses to prevent political reabsorption in the expanding community,[13] partly to avoid sharing the costs of maintaining an obsolescent physical structure and partly to exercise selectivity in what uses may occupy their lands. In that event the once inclusive government of a locality faces increasingly serious fiscal problems. But where local government autonomy is relatively centralized, outlying localities have no political administrative instrument with which to oppose annexation. Accordingly, the administrative boundaries of an expanding community can be extended to include the centrifugally moving units. But while local polities are trying to resolve the problems of discrepant boundaries, the issue arises repeatedly in larger theaters.

Because much of what occurs within political boundaries is determined by events taking place within the ambits of systemic boundaries, a polity always tends to enlarge its political boundary to correspond more closely to its systemic boundary. One approach is to merge communal polities into provincial polities and those into state polities. On some occasions such extensions have been pushed to the farthest extremities of an ecosystem. But the burden of administering and policing an entire ecosystem has proven insuperable. Overexpansion is the rock on which many a ship of ancient empire foundered. A more important limiting condition, especially in the modern period, is the circumstance that much of the regional and interregional areas over which a given system is extended falls within the domains of other polities. Systems overlap and interpenetrate to such a degree that no one can claim territorial sovereignty over ecosystem scope. What Pappenfort found for metropolitan-based systems is no less true of state-based systems. Nevertheless, polities continue to try to bring larger portions of system territories under their jurisdictions. When military means prove too costly, as has been the experience of modern imperialistic states, resort is had to marketing and financial persuasions.[14]

The overreaching of polity boundaries by ecosystems is most commonly accomplished through the establishment of trading relations among corporate units located in different political territories. In addition, there may be an exportation of capital from one polity to another, either as a direct loan or as an investment in a foreign enterprise. That may be followed by the location in other political areas of branch plants or by the acquisition through purchase of plants native to those areas. The multinational corporation is a prime example of that mode of system extension. Further system interpenetration occurs as local chapters of categoric units enter into multinational federations. A recent count of categoric units with branches in three or more national states showed a total in excess of twenty-two thousand (*Yearbook of International Organizations* 1984). Linkages, such as religious affiliations and artistic and intellectual exchange arrangements, may develop along still other lines. A thickening of the network through these several means makes the exercise of autonomy by any one polity increasingly difficult. Indications of a supra- or multinational polity begin to surface, as represented by the United Nations and treaty organizations.

An international network of linkages is built of symbiotic and commensal relations, as are networks of lesser scope. Functional differences, among which symbiotic relations form, are both substantive and ordinal. Consequently, the network assumes hierarchical form. A key function in the international hierarchy derives from possession of a rich resource base, an organization capable of employing a highly developed technology, and an unrestricted access to information flows. Attempts to define strata in the hierarchy have revolved around, for the most part, a threefold categorization, namely, core, semiperipheral, and peripheral nations (Wallerstein 1974). It is entirely possible, of course, that so simple a conception is but a first approximation.[15] Although commensal relations may lie mainly in the strata, some also fall across strata bounds. As in any imperfect system, such relations tend to be fluid; they form around specific issues and dissolve as these issues disappear, only to form again around different issues.

The ability to enter effectively into the networks that spring up among autonomous polities is governed to some extent, ceteris paribus, by size of polity. Small states lack the resources and capital that would enable them to enjoy economies of scale in production. Thus they are competitively disadvantaged. For much the same reason, they are unable to support extensive diplomatic relations abroad or large military establishments at home (Vital 1967; Robinson 1963; Sawyer 1967).

Still, inequalities among nation-states are only partly affected by size differences. Other influential factors include the point in a nation-state's history at which it entered the international universe of discourse, the role performed in international trade, and the degree to which unification as a polity has been achieved. Inferiority in these respects has been described as underdevelopment; that, in turn, has found contrasting explanations. On the one hand, underdevelopment is viewed as incomplete modernization. That is to say, the structural transformation needed for the effective mobilization of capital and its employment in productive industries with all that that implies about divestiture of inhibiting folkways, the extension of literacy, and the cultivation of entrepreneurial skills has not been accomplished.

An opposing explanation, on the other hand, appears in what is known as "dependency theory," which argues that "the economies of one group of countries are conditioned by the development and expansion of others in such a way that the development of the former is blocked" (Dos Santos 1973, 73). The blockage is attributed to the exploitative nature of capitalism, which has held underdeveloped countries in the positions of raw material producers and preserves their dependence on industrialized, developed countries. Consequently, so runs the argument, population distribution is over-urbanized (Kanter 1981); service sectors grow disproportionally (Portes 1979; Evans and Timberlake 1980); economic inequalities are widened (Rubinson 1976; Chase-Dunn 1975); and democracy fails to develop (Bollen 1983).

Whereas the modernization theory is guilty of naïve optimism, the ideological predilection of the dependency theory blinds it to important historical and economic facts (Ley 1982). Both engage in oversimplifications. The former fails to give sufficient attention to internal structural factors, affected in no small degree by prior colonial status, and to position in the international ecosystem. On their part, dependency theorists seldom recognize historical precedents, for example, that all major organizational transformations in societies have proceeded unevenly. That economic inequalities tend to increase before an institutional framework is developed that can reduce the differential seems to have been the rule (Williamson 1965). Nor do dependency theorists seem aware of the theoretical probability that inequality among polities might well be an unavoidable condition of an international division of labor, whether built upon private or state capitalist principles.[16]

Lacking a supranational polity, the hierarchy of state polities is subject to instability. Despite the inertia that infects hierarchies, the creation of worldwide communication linkages and the resulting diffusion of knowledge sooner or later provoke challenges to the dominant polities. Any subdominant polity that can marshal the requisite resources can tap into networks and share in information flows. Where resources are meager, collusive action on the part of two or more polities can be used to pool resources. By that means, dominance over the many by the few can be reduced. Such combines, however, are themselves unstable. The suppression of divergent interests to meet a particular threat lasts only so long as the threat exists.

In sum, three quite general effects of the maturation of a regional and interregional division of labor are to be noted. First, the biophysical environments of each formerly semi-independent system are merged in a single biophysical environment from which all draw sustenance. Second, whereas the once semi-independent systems were, while in that state, environmental to one another, the expansion process converts them to a status of subsystems in a more inclusive system. Third, system growth absorbs an increasing proportion of the ecumenic environment into the system.

PROPOSITIONAL RÉSUMÉ

Assumptions

5-A1   Increases in area and population incidental to cumulative change vary with reductions in mobility costs.

5-A2   The distributions of population and the units of its organization in space are shaped by mobility costs.

Hypotheses

5-H1   Cumulative change begins at route intersections and proceeds through a series of phases including:

5-H1.1   an extension of linear (radial) routes to outlying settlements, establishing a rudimentary division of labor;

5-H1.2   growth and reorganization of the settlement at the central node sufficient to support and administer an enlarged network of relations;

5-H1.3   elaboration of a linkage network in a region, further development of a territorial division of labor, and a conversion of outlying systems to subsystems in an expanded system;

5-H1.4   progressive centralization of control and an ordering of subsystems in a hierarchy of size and number of specialized functions.

5-H2   The boundary of an ecosystem falls at the isoline though the points at which the value of goods and services exchanged with a center falls below the costs of transportation to the center.

5-H3   Interrelated units distribute themselves in time and space with reference to the frequency of interactions among them; that is, a spatial pattern is a diagram of a temporal pattern.

5-H3.1   The greater the number of units operating per interval of time, the more fully utilized is the time span of the diurnal cycle, that is, the closer the approximation to an arhythmic flow of activity in the system.

5-H4   Mobility costs in an area of regional scope vary on a U-shaped curve with density of time-space occupance.

5-H4.1   The higher the mobility costs, the greater is the tendency for operating and control functions to occur at the same site.

5-H4.2   As mobility costs decline, the covariation between the locations of operating and control functions shifts from direct to inverse to random.

5-H4.3   The lower the mobility costs, the lower the accessibility value of proximity among interrelated units.

5-H5   As the costs of short-distance (intramural) mobility decline, units distribute themselves on a gradient from a transportation node such that their distances removed varies inversely with their intensities of use of time and space.

5-H5.1   The more specialized the unit, the lower is its tolerance for location variability.

5-H5.2   The greater the similarity of units, the greater the tendency to concentrate at given locations.

5-H5.3   The higher the social–economic status of residents, the greater the tendency for a segregation of residences and a dispersion of daily travel destinations to vary inversely.

5-H5.4   Reductions in mobility costs result in a substitution of commuting (recurrent) movements for residence changes (nonrecurrent movements).

5-H6   Reductions in mobility costs convert semi-independent systems into subsystems in a more inclusive ecosystem.

5-H7   A sequence of changes in the territorial distribution of units whose functions comprise a system is repeated to the extent that a given series of changes in transportation and communication technology is repeated.

5-H8   Polities always tend to extend their boundaries to make them coterminous with the boundaries of the ecosystem.

5-H9   The principle of hierarchy applies to territorially differentiated agglomerations as well as to functions and subsystems in an ecosystem.

6

Limits to

Cumulative Change

The exponential increase of information and mechanical applications has been repeatedly documented.[1] It is also true that the scale and complexity of the human ecosystem has grown at an accelerating rate, if not on an exponential curve. The overreaching of national polities by manifold interrelations is already so far advanced that some scholars are able to speak of a world system. This raises a question of whether there are limits to cumulative change. Does the process approach an equilibrium state in which few, if any, functions and organizations of functions can be added to a structure? Is there, for example, an analogy between ecosystem change and the fermentation process? In the latter, it will be recalled, in a given solution the proportion of alcohol produced by bacterial action reaches a level such that the bacteria can no longer survive in the solution, with the result that fermentation ceases. If there is more than a faint resemblance between the two processes, what is the alcohol counterpart in a changing ecosystem? And is the chemistry the same regardless of the scale on which a system is mounted; does a world system behave in the same manner as a localized or regional system?

Conceivably limits to cumulative change might arise from any of various circumstances. They might be found in the increasing pressure of population on finite resource supplies. Or limits might be implicit in one or more kinds of organizational processes, such as nonproportionality in the changes among components of structure, excessive organizational density, structural discontinuities, or a loss of diversity in the movement toward isomorphism. I shall comment on each of these possibilities.

Biophysical Environment

An elemental argument put forth in a Club of Rome report titled *The Limits to Growth* (Meadows et al. 1972) holds that any given rate of resource use will in time lead to an exhaustion of a fixed supply and that unchecked population growth will shorten that time. The basic premise of that argument, namely, that the biophysical environment is finite, is incontrovertible. That environment is confined to the earth and an atmospheric envelope of measurable extent. While some of the components are renewable, for example, plant and animal life, others are not. Renewability, moreover, is confined to the durations of life cycles and to the maintenance of vital networks in the biosphere. There is a fragility as well as a finiteness in the biophysical environment. The question posed by these facts is: Do they determine carrying capacity for human population and through that for system scale and complexity? Have the 4.5 billion people in the world, having nearly doubled in the three decades since 1950, approached the limit imposed by an inelastic resource base?

The notion of environmental finitude presupposes a resource inventory. But what should enter into an inventory changes over time. So also does the feasibility of preparing an inventory. On both counts the end product is subject to technological restraints in both the mechanical and the organizational senses of the term. Technological advances have produced a long history of resource substitutions, of bronze for flint stones, iron for bronze, aluminum and manganese for iron. Plastics have replaced metals in many uses; chemical fertilizers have substituted for land; and energy is replacing materials (cf. Goeller and Weinberg 1976, 683–86). Substitutions, of course, are not always complete. The employment of a new resource often relegates an old resource to a lesser or a different use. Technological advance has spread resource usage over a widening variety of materials, not a few of which have long been in use.

A resource inventory also relies heavily on the available techniques for detection and measurement. Developments in electromagnetism have helped locate iron deposits, advances in geology and seismic surveying have led to the identification of oil domes, and various kinds of remote sensing with the aid of satellites have made possible the scanning of large areas for metallic deposits (Gould 1976). Known supplies have been extended by technical advances, as in the recovery of oil from old wells by water injection and the uses of low-grade ores by electrolytic refining processes.

Resource scarcity is relative to demand. And demand manifests itself in price. Price, in turn, is an amalgam of capital costs, exploration costs, transportation costs, processing costs, and marketing costs and is subject to consumer tolerance. Price may be artificially inflated by monopoly, oligopoly, and customs barriers. Likewise the costs of technically feasible explorations may be raised by licensing claims issuing from ownership or sovereignty. Thus although price may be the most effective measure of scarcity, it measures relative rather than absolute scarcity, that is, availability. The measurement problem is aptly stated by Mishan (1977, 65): "The best we can do today is to infer tentatively from highly limited global models using controversial assumptions about future technological progress and about world reserves of materials, that growth at present rates, either of population or of industrial output, cannot continue for more than a century."

It is noteworthy that in a technologically sophisticated economy, such as that of the United States, the ratio of net national product to costs of materials used, including food, energy, and physical materials, has followed a linear increase through all of the century, 1847–1957, for which the curve has been plotted (Kendrick 1961, 95–97; Barnett and Morse 1963, 199). Furthermore, the per capita amount of materials consumed, exclusive of food and energy, appears to have remained constant in the two decades following 1952 (Landsberg 1976, 637). A separate computation involving energy alone shows that that, too, has declined per capita. Further reductions in energy costs are resulting from rapid advances in electronics technology. To what extent the diffusion of technology will spread such effects over the developing as well as the developed areas of the world remains to be seen.

A critical element in the support capability of the biophysical environment for population is the volume of food-producing resources. Contrary to the neo-Malthusian prophecies of doom (Hardin 1968; Ehrlich 1968; Masering, 1976),[2] careful examination of sources has shown that the available arable land in the world is approximately twice the amount actually in use (Barnett and Morse 1963; Walters 1975; Ravelle 1976; Simon 1980); that productivity per hectare and the aggregate amount of product have increased more or less continuously since 1961–62 (Walters 1975); and that an annual increase of agricultural product of 3.5 to 4.0 percent per year is both technologically and economically feasible (Murdoch 1980, 133). Murdoch's estimate of increased productivity is nearly twice as high as population growth rates in the rapidly growing parts of the world. Productivity increases have drawn more heavily on energy reserves directly, through the use of chemical fertilizers, and indirectly in the manufacture of capital equipment. As energy consumption has increased, labor input has declined (Steinhart and Steinhart 1974). The net effect is a declining cost per unit of product.[3]

Despite resource availability and progress in productivity, there are areas of the world subject to chronic food shortages. The problem has its roots in poverty. And poverty is embedded in a mesh of organizational circumstances, the composition of which varies from place to place. They include such conditions as primitive transportation and communication facilities, insufficient credit and marketing services, land costs and exploitative rents, pricing practices, government instability and the flight of capital, a scarcity of administrative experience, and other institutional rigidities. Structural conditions such as these operate independently of resource supplies.

In sum, resource supplies are not unlike Einsteinian space: finite but unbounded.

Ecosystem Structures

Population and the Ecosystem

The demographic counterpart of improvements in food supplies is an increasing life expectancy at birth, which is perhaps the most sensitive of all indicators of general welfare. Life expectancy has advanced from around thirty years in the preindustrial period to approximately seventy or more years in the modern developed countries and to fifty or more years in the developing parts of the world, exclusive of Africa south of the Sahara. Some increases can be attributed to improvements in medical and sanitary knowledge and their worldwide dissemination. Yet it is doubtful that reductions in mortality by such means can be sustained without improved nutrition.[4]

As longevity is extended, intrinsic growth rates of population subside. Births are replaced by added years of life. That is, where the expectancy of life is on the order of seventy years, each birth yields more than twice the realized years than where life expectancy is around thirty years. The greater life span is more economical in that it allows both a longer period of training of the young and a work life of forty years instead of the no more than twenty years formerly realized. Thus age-standardized fertility and mortality rates return to a mere replacement level. This, however, as mentioned earlier, is not an end to population growth. The large number of youths produced in the tardy decline of fertility are themselves producers of many offspring, even though their rates of reproduction are at replacement levels. For the large number of reproducers to age out of the population and for overall growth to cease, another thirty to fifty years must pass.

Age-composition changes incidental to a declining growth rate affects not only the numbers of reproducers. Maturation to reproducing ages is also an advance to labor force entry ages. Rapid increase in the size of the labor force age population may exceed the increases in employment opportunities, a disproportion that can become very acute when sharp declines in mortality occur. Youths are brought into competition with members of the parental generation for leadership positions of all kinds as well as for positions in the economy. In the meantime the aging process gradually removes older workers from the labor force and builds a growing proportion of superannuated dependents.

Clearly the relation of population numbers to the biophysical environment in a technologically advanced system eludes any simple explanation. The matter is further complicated by changes in the internal organization of particular populations. For example, as the ratio of capital to labor continues on its rising curve, as has been the experience in the United States

(Abramowitz 1956, 8; Solow 1957; Bowen and Mangum 1966; Kendrick 1973, 124), the relative size of the employed labor force tends to decline (Long 1958, 146). The decline is obscured somewhat by the progressive transfer of workers from unpaid to paid categories, inasmuch as most official censuses count only the latter as members of the labor force. The decline may also be postponed by political pressures to create new forms of work to accommodate outsized cohorts passing through an age structure or to admit to the labor force members of minority groups that have been held in labor reserves. After these adjustments have been made, the secular decline in labor force size may be expected to resume.

Accordingly, population size tends to become a neutral factor in the growth and development of the producing sector of a system (Hirschman 1958, 181). And that feeds back upon the population replacement rate. Saunders and Rinehart (1967) have shown that the association of replacement rates with energy consumption is strongly negative when consumption is low and drops to zero when consumption reaches two thousand kilograms per capita. It has been said once before that system development produces organizational equivalents of population.

Still a relative decline of the labor force requirement does not in itself call for a reduction of population size. The role of persons as consumers remains important, possibly increasingly important. A maintenance of scale economies and an associated standard of living requires enough consumption to support a continuing rate of production. For that to occur the aggregate income of workers must increase at least to an extent equal to what would have been the aggregate income of workers withdrawn from production. Increase in productivity per worker can more than compensate for increase in the nonworking population.

Furthermore, while the birth-death balance at the beginning of the demographic transition is indicative of a population-organization equilibrium, a similar inference cannot be drawn from the return to a birth-death balance at the end of the growth cycle. For just as productivity in particular systems tends to become independent of population size, so technical accumulation also seems to follow a curve that becomes independent of the number of people. In fact, knowledge acquisition, coupled with mechanical and electronic information storage and retrieval facilities, enables knowledge to increase faster than its utilization. Organizational complexity is unchecked by population size.

At the core of the return to a demographic equilibrium and its implications for the population-system relationship is the fact that the population of a bounded polity, for example, a nation-state, loses its utility for purposes of delimiting a system. With the increasing density of interregional relations, their several populations are in effect merged in a supraregional or suprastate population. Market expansion substitutes for local population increase, and technical advances in each region build upon those made in all other regions. As that occurs, the ecumenic environment is absorbed into the inclusive system, for the former local and regional systems are converted to subsystems in a world system. Although this might seem to restore the biophysical environment to a paramount position vis-à-vis the comprehensive ecosystem, its effects must still be filtered through many layers of organization. Structural limits to change will probably be reached well before resource supplies are reduced to critical levels.

Increases in population size, together with increases in the production and use of nondegradable materials, unquestionably pose a threat to the preservation of quality in the biophysical environment. But how a deterioration of quality, short of a nuclear holocaust, would affect cumulative change is a question that cannot be satisfactorily answered in the present state of knowledge. The lack of adequate trend data on pollutants, of dependable assessments of their effects, and of consensus on standards to be adopted in their regulation postpones any conclusion about eventual outcomes (Stokinger 1971). Far from impeding structural growth, pollution control requires further increments to growth. Controls cannot be effectively implemented on a local, regional, or even a continental basis. Nothing short of the creation of a central organization with requisite monitoring, reporting, and enforcing powers can prevent the contamination of rivers and seas, the airborne spread of particulates from combustion and the resulting acid rain, or a random dumping of radioactive wastes. Structure, it seems, begets structure.

Nonproportional Change

The most general statement of a structural limitation to growth has been put forth by Boulding (1953). He declared that the maximum size of a structure is fixed by its inability to compensate for nonproportional changes among its parts. Nonproportionality was described earlier as resulting from an exponential increase in relations accompanying a linear or arithmetic increase in functions. It was also noted that the congestion implied in an exponential increase in relations is attenuated in part by the substitution of intercategory for interindividual relations and, perhaps more important, by the formation of complex units. The latter channel materials and information to specialists who distill their content and transmit the products through sequences of linkages to much larger populations. But there are limits, says Boulding, to the extent that complex units can perform that function. The parameter assumed to be relatively constant is the efficiency of the technology for mobility. In consequence, blockages arise at critical junctures in the system, due in part to excessive centralization and in part to a superfluity of rules and regulatory arrangements.

In other words, advances in complexity of ecosystems may develop an organizational density that raises communication and transportation costs to near prohibitive levels. That has often been the experience in localized ecosystems wherein technical improvements have failed to keep pace with agglomeration trends. Some modern evidence of that is found in the deconcentration of the components of large metropolitan centers in Western nations.

But the rigidities in mobility technology assumed in the nonproportional hypothesis may be unwarranted. In the electronic era, for example, the costs of information transmission and storage are steadily reduced. With the appearance of instantaneous communication, the element of time as a cost has been virtually eliminated, barring short periods of overloading. Risks of overload have been undergoing dramatic reduction through broadened bandwidth of transmission lines. A single glass fiber, no larger than a human hair, can carry eight hundred voice conversations, or fifty thousand bits of information, per second. Hundreds of such fibers can be combined in a single cable (Branscomb 1979, 146). With more extensive applications of electronic circuitry the storage and retrieval of information from memory banks is also subject to significant technical advances. Material costs per unit of information are now approaching a negligible figure.

The conveyance of people and goods has not enjoyed cost

reductions comparable to those in communication, for unlike information, tangible things have weight and bulk. Even so, the cost trend has been downward. That has followed in part the substitution of communication for transportation in many kinds of transactions. Reduction of transport costs has also resulted from the uses of lighter materials in vehicle construction, more efficient power units, and larger payload capacities of carriers. Yet most of the cost reductions apply on a per ton-mile basis. It may still be that the volume of goods and persons to be moved may offset the gains made in speeding cargo flows. That trend may be expected to continue rising as increasing proportions of the world's population are brought into full participation in the ecumene. Congestion of ports and rail and air terminals could nullify gains in efficiency elsewhere in the system. It is probable, however, that further advances in computer-controlled schedules of deliveries and cargo handling will alleviate congestion. In the meantime, mobility costs arising from congestion will tend to be more characteristic of particular systems than of an inclusive world system. It is well known that the frequency of exchange declines on a gradient with distance from transportation nodes. The slope of the gradient will remain relatively steep as long as there is unevenness in the participation of subsystems in a world system.

Accumulation of Niche Closures

The root cause of nonproportionality may lie elsewhere, according to Mancur Olson (1982, 36–72). He argues that in large stable systems with unchanging boundaries, collusive organization in special interest categories multiply. Since the costs of contributing to a public good seldom yield commensurate returns to the members of such categoric units, they rarely act in the public interest except where it happens to coincide with the private interest. As every avenue of action that might lead to a public good is commandeered by a special interest unit, flexibility in the system wanes and the prospect for further change diminishes. An equilibrium composed of countervailing inertias, however, may depend on a greater degree of closure in a system than normally exists. Olson's assumed stability may be no more than temporary. More than one categoric unit has had its foothold undermined by technical developments, for example, the brotherhoods of railway workers. Foreign competition can displace a domestic industry and strand its occupational categories in obsolescence. In general the conditions that foster the growth of a system are also the sources of disturbances in the system.

The obverse side of the Olson proposition is manifested in the centrifugal tendencies generated with increases of organization scale. Special interest units are no more exempt from scale effects than are the systems in which they arise. With growth in size, the special interest unit becomes increasingly occupied with matters of general concern, and it loses its ability to attend to all of the special preoccupations of its members. Thus it departmentalizes, and each step in that direction weakens its integration. Centrifugal tendencies of this order belong largely to categoric units. Their reliance on crisis to refocus attention on the common interest leaves them vulnerable to segmentation when crises are absent. Corporate units, on the other hand, are able to harness centrifugal forces. As further subdivisions of specialized functions occur, they are assigned appropriate positions in the corporate hierarchy to which specific responsibilities are delegated. It is still possible, however, for a centrifugal force to operate among the functions of corporate units. A separation of the production of tangible goods (products) from intangible goods (profits) tends to occur when the preoccupations with finance lead to a sharing of control with credit agencies. That can mark the demise of the unit as an effective competitor in a product market.

Centrifugal tendencies may work differently in a system of ecosystems. Without the support of a network of symbiotic relations, a simple unification of polities in an empire tends to be unstable. The problems of survival mount as scope is increased, especially where there is no corresponding improvement in communications. Efficient communications, however, give no assurance of lasting solidarity in collusive arrangements among polities. There, too, special interests drive wedges into the fibers of mutual aid agreements. The wedges are forged in the imperatives of functional interdependence. Whether a network of interdependences can attain a unity comparable to that of a corporate unit is uncertain. It lacks the centralization of authority needed to maintain the parts in assigned positions. The parts are not ordered in transitive sequences. Their interrelations more nearly resemble the spokes of many overlapping wheels.

Inelasticities in Positional Goods

It has been suggested that the march toward complexity brings to the surface another kind of structural limitation. An increasing abundance of material goods, assuming a reduction of inequalities in their distribution, does not affect the scarcity of positional goods, as Hirsch (1976, 27–39) has contended. No matter how affluent on a per capita basis a population may be, there are but a limited number of leadership positions, choice residential sites, and other status items. No subsystem needs more than one key functionary, a universally high level of educational attainment notwithstanding, and a coast line offers no more than a few residential locations with beautiful vistas. But there is greater elasticity in the supply of positional goods than Hirsch seems to realize. The potential number of categoric units, each offering one or more status positions, is legion. Who has counted the number of committee chairmanships in the faculty of a large university? Furthermore, the practice of prescribing tenure for positions spreads access to such goods even more widely in a population. Again, if the principal measure of a positional good is status, another path to its attainment is through the amassing of material goods.

On a larger scale the hierarchical ordering of local polities or nations also comprises a limited number of ordinal positions. Although all can have free access to interregional trade, not all can enjoy equality of positions on scales of size, resources, or centrality relative to information flows. Hierarchy on functional grounds seems as unavoidable in a socialist as in a capitalist context. The positional shifts resulting from technological changes and the consequent alteration of resource values may not change the number of status positions. Here again, however, the creation of international control organizations can greatly multiply nominal status positions among nations. Functional differentiation constitutes a framework that supports numerous categoric alignments with their respective positional goods.

The unanswered question is: How important are positional goods? Do their benefits equal their costs in the form of responsibilities and inconveniences? The question may find different answers in the various segments of a population. All things considered, however, it seems that there are no proximate limits on the amount of positional goods.

Structural Discontinuities

Another way of looking at some of the limiting circumstances mentioned thus far is as structural imperfections. There is no basis for assuming that any given system is complete in its composition or that its organization is entirely coherent. A system, in fact, may include one or more disjunctures, which can impede further cumulative change. The persistence, for example, of folk practices beyond their relevance to current needs distorts when it does not prevent growth. One of the most virulent anachronisms is the reliance upon kinship obligations in the distribution of preferments. Nepotism begets nepotism until an entire system is threatened with stagnation. A more institutionalized practice is the custom of apprenticeship, which becomes obstructive when carried from a guild organization in a handicraft economy to a mechanized, industrial economy (Ashton 1964, 77; Smelser 1959, 104–5).

The history of technological change offers numerous instances of stops and starts owing to uneven information inputs. More visible to the observer of history is the absence of necessary functional units. A lagging development of transportation and communication denies a system the degree of integration required for economies of scale. Or, if transportation is available but information-distributing facilities are lacking, producers are handicapped in efforts to make market comparisons. But even with adequate means for the movement of products and information, their uses can be restricted by the lack of appropriate credit facilities. The development of missing pieces in a system in transformation can be long delayed by instabilities in a central government. Capital flees the area, and technology is starved of the wherewithal for its application. On the other hand, if stability in government is attained through the monopolization of control by a small clique, it may offer as great a deterrence to cumulative change as does instability. Excessive concentration of power can be as potent a barrier to development as can an entirely even distribution over all special interest groups. Increasing complexity brings with it mounting problems of exercising necessary regulatory powers, independent of the degree of power concentration. Problems of acquiring the knowledge required for policy implementation, of dealing with unanticipated consequences of policy applications, and of reconciling conflicting interests tax even the most modern of governments (Greer 1979, 315).

Structural discontinuities are greatly magnified when attention shifts from a localized system to an international or world system. For various historical reasons, different parts of the world have developed unevenly. As a result the task of designing workable measures of governance is extremely difficult. It is not even certain that administrative and political lessons learned within polities are transferable to an interpolity government.

Convergence, Isomorphism, and Information Accumulation

Structural isomorphism among subsystems growing out of developmental convergence was discussed earlier as a necessary concomitant of within-system complexity. Lacking structural comparability, subsystems can communicate only with great difficulty. Growth and even survival is problematic. But structural isomorphism without functional differentiation is antithetical to cumulative change. Subsystems identical in both function and structure have nothing to exchange. Their only operating relation is a competitive one. Fortunately for an ecosystem, that circumstance is confined within functional categories or niches.

Nevertheless, it is not unlikely that the trend toward convergence in structure and process among the parts of a world system may progressively dampen the rate of change. Interstimulation subsists on the occurrence of unique experiences. Thus if all degrees of relative isolation are removed such that unique experiences rarely occur, no one subsystem can learn anything from another. In that unlikely event, the externalities essential to change will have disappeared.

Slowed though the rate of change may be, its end would seem to be a remote probability. There are imperfections in communication that make for degrees of isolation at various points in a network. Imperfections are traceable to differences in wealth and to the exigencies of territorial specialization. Even though access to the total fund of information may be unrestricted in principle, not all subsystems will be able to or have reason to assimilate the totality of that fund.

There is yet another circumstance that could forestall an end to cumulative change. That exists in the vast fund of information that has already accumulated in the repositories of the world. Until the combination and recombination of the items of information in that resource have exhausted all possibilities, change will continue. That such a prospect is practicable lies in the remote future. The preponderating role of information in current system change introduces a large element of unpredictability in the process (Boulding 1975, 324). Where and when the process will surge again is difficult to know. And since the incidence of new syntheses may be expected to occur in random distribution about the world, the elements of externality reappear for each and every individual location. The random incidence of information syntheses might be expected to intrude upon and divert isomorphic tendencies.

There is also the probability that limits to exploration on the frontiers of knowledge will develop well before the potential number of new syntheses approaches exhaustion. A growing awareness in the public that scientific discovery may carry undesirable social and ethical implications is giving rise to demands for accountability from scientists (cf. Morison 1978). That experimentations with recombinant DNA, uses of human subjects in biological research, and work with fissionable materials yielding nondegradable toxic wastes should not be permitted to go forward without oversight by responsible agencies of the public is gaining a widening acceptance. A new kind of externality has appeared on the threshold of science, the import of which is to check and possibly redirect rather than to promote investigation. As in other spheres of system functioning, the control over its activity by scientists must now be shared by the presumed beneficiaries of the product. But this kind of resistance to research explorations could be as random in occurrence as are the information syntheses produced by research.

In any case, it is likely that a point might be reached at which an accumulation of information syntheses ceases to have any effect on organizational complexity. A high degree of complexity may be able to accommodate an indeterminate amount of technical and intellectual lore. The effects of accumulation then may be to substitute new forms of organization for old. Gains may be realized in efficiency, in aesthetics, in equity, or in all three; the shift may be to quality rather than to quantity. Evolution would then take on a new coloration and a new direction.

Conclusion

My review of propositions concerning sources of limits to cumulative change has failed to reveal a clear analog to the alcohol factor in the fermentation process. Every promising suggestion rests upon a ceteris paribus assumption, namely, that a system has attained so high a degree of closure that all relevant parameters are contained within specifiable bounds. While that might be acceptable for analytical purposes when dealing with localized systems, it is not acceptable on any other grounds. Approaches to asymptotes are invariably offset by compensatory influences arising from outside localized systems.

So the question must be phrased anew for an inclusive or world system. In principle it would seem that all of the limiting circumstances that tend to arise in one level of organization—nonproportional change, multiplication of countervailing special interest groups, structural discontinuities, and structural convergence—would have to be reasserted at a higher level of organization. But knowability in the latter case is fraught with uncertainty. Still, the degrees of freedom for cumulative change would seem to be fewer in an inclusive system and therefore might eventually be exhausted. Thus it might well be that limiting effects develop in the alternating swings, perhaps in a Markov pattern, from structural discontinuity to structural convergence. But this reckons without a full understanding of the implications of an exponential accumulation of information.

PROPOSITIONAL RÉSUMÉ

Assumption

3-H3.1 The efficiency of transportation and communication technology limits ecosystem complexity.

Hypotheses

6-H1 Limiting effects of biophysical environment on cumulative change assumes ecosystem closure.

6-H2 The effect of population size and composition on cumulative change in any given system is neutralized as scale of system is increased.

6-H3 The locus of structural limits to cumulative change shifts from local to regional to interregional scale.

6-H4 The principal sources of limits to cumulative change, regardless of ecosystem scale, alternate between structural discontinuities and structural convergences.

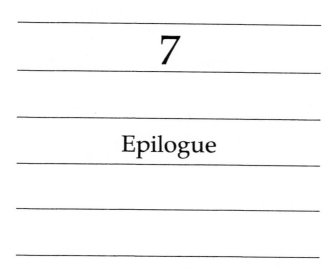

7

Epilogue

Ecology and Human Ecology

I began this volume with a textbook definition of ecology as the study of the relation of organisms to environment. That, I maintain, is the one point of agreement, the common denominator, among all of the several intellectual preoccupations that are characterized by their proponents as ecology. One may go further to add that all also view the organism-environment relation as adaptive, though for some, adaptation is regarded as an end state, while among others it is viewed as a process. Beyond that point, consensus is compromised in one way or another.

Although it accepts the covering definition of the field of study, human ecology begins its departure in the postulates laid down to define the human individual. These were stated as five in number, namely, a necessity for environmental access, inescapable interdependence, inherent expansiveness, temporal constraint, and a variability of behavior with indeterminate limits. All but the last of these are shared with all classes of living things. But the last one opens wide the door to divergences of the human from other species in the implications the other postulates have for the kind of environmental relation established.

Divergences are numerous. They appear in the recognition

of an environment beyond the biophysical, in the inutility of the species concept, in the modes of energy circulation through the ecosystem hierarchy, in the incidence of vertical mobility, in the view of selectivity as exercised by the ecosystem rather than by environment, in the power of cumulative change, in the formation of complex units, and in still other ways. Consequently the human ecologist is led away from the models employed in bioecology. That finds its fullest expression in the commitment to organization as the adaptive mechanism.

I do not wish to say, however, that there are no theoretical lessons to be learned from the more general discipline. The history of human ecology documents many borrowings from its predecessor, many fruitful, some not. A liaison with bioecology will continue to prove useful in the future as it has in the past. The wise human ecologist will browse widely in the literature of bioecology, for there are to be found many researches based on propositions and assumptions congenial to the needs of human ecology. Still, human ecology must draw out the implications of its assumptions and test the inferences with data from human collective life without expecting, to say nothing of demanding, close parallels with the models and conclusions of bioecology.

The basic assumption of human ecology, to repeat, is that adaptation is a collective rather than an individual process. And that in turn commits the point of view to a macrolevel approach. Such an approach is confined to properties and conditions that cannot be distributed to individuals (Carlsson 1968), in other words, system properties. These comprise the principal parameters of collective life. As such they describe a structure of relations that channel and circumscribe all individual activity.

It is on this point that human ecology is most often misunderstood. Contrary to some allegations, a macrolevel approach is not deterministic in a mechanical sense as Carroll (1984, 1) has said, unless the expectation of cause and effect is determinism. The use of the term *natural* in the early literature to describe the workings of factor interactions was unfortunate. It seemed to imply that outcomes were automatic (Berry and Kasarda 1977, 353, 413). But the propositions set forth in chapter résumés are all conceived in probabilistic terms. Inevitability is as foreign to human ecology as human ecology is to Greek drama.

It becomes desirable, therefore, to exorcise the notion of competition as a generalized causal principle for complex phenomena, for that has been the conceptual peg on which the "natural" and "automatic" cloaks have been hung. As a Malthusian-Darwinian heritage, competition is not only a great oversimplification, its falsifiability is questionable. The term pertains to a situation in which individuals or other units are making demands upon a common resource in excess of the quantity of that resource. As a type of relation, competition is readily observable; as a producer of particular outcomes it is obscure. At most it helps account for the elimination of some contestants from a share of the limited resource. It does not, however, shed any light on what happens to the excluded members of a population after their exclusion. Other independent variables must be introduced to explain subsequent events. Furthermore, a preoccupation with competition fails to recognize the occurrence of noncompeting populations. Some populations are so unlike in their resource requirements that their interactions are symbiotic from the outset rather than a result from an earlier competition. Trading partners fall into that category, as do physicians and plumbers, accountants and carpenters, and many species of lower forms of life (cf. Strong et al. 1984, 54–66, 67–100).

A macrolevel approach does not deny that the human individual engages in motivated and evaluative activity. It is rather that data pertaining to such aspects of behavior are simply not used where the primary concern is with populations. A distinction between anticipated and unanticipated events is not useful in that context. The consequences of action are what are important at the macrolevel. I have made these points before, and I repeat them now only because they are pertinent to a particular issue.

That issue has to do with the place of policy in ecological phenomena. It is generally the case that ecologists do not confront policy matters directly. On the other hand, advocates of a political economy approach to structural change (Walton 1979; Roberts 1978; Portes 1979) cast policy in a primary role. That, in turn, leads them to give considerable weight to both the purposes of individuals (e.g., capitalists) and to ideologies and value systems of societies (e.g., capitalism, socialism). But one would like to know under what conditions policies appear and how effective they may be in overriding ecological principles.

Human Ecology and Social Policy

Policies may be classified on the basis of their intended effect relative to change. They may be designed to preserve a status quo by excluding change, to reverse a change in process, to accommodate a change under way, or to produce a desirable change.

Policy designed to prevent change or a certain kind of change appears for the most part in relatively isolated or parochial systems. Despotic governments have usually sought to exclude change by prohibiting movements of people across their frontiers. The assumption, correctly enough, has been that an infusion of ideas and experiences from abroad carries criticisms and threats to the established order. Nevertheless, even though external contacts may be confined to bearers of luxury goods and monopolized by an elite, the trader invariably brings with him or her the stuff of innovation. The difficulties of containing innovation mount with improvements in transportation and communication.

A more current example of contrachange policy is seen in the anti–birth control posture of the Catholic church hierarchy. Before widespread declines in mortality occurred, such a policy was inconceivable. Once that decline began and proved irreversible, however, the birth rate eventually followed the same course, for the birth rate normally seeks the level of the death rate. The Vatican's pronatalist policy fails to recognize that fact. Hence its opposition has accomplished little more than slowing the pace of fertility decline among its members. The Latin American experience is especially instructive on this point: nearly universal Catholicism has not prevented fertility decline in every country (Kirk 1971). Parenthetically, there is no known instance of success in attempts to reverse declining fertility where mortality has remained low.

Policy conceived for the purpose of reversing change already in process is well illustrated by the efforts of a number of third world countries to stem internal migration flows to their metropolitan centers. Various methods have been employed to achieve that end, such as requiring residence permits for settlement in destination cities, redistributing economic opportunities to "growth-pole" towns (sites of potential development) in interiors of countries, and instituting land reform programs to attach potential migrants to land plots. The record thus far, as reported by Laquian and Simmons (1979) and Simmons (1979), varies from outright failure to qualified success. The poor results are traceable to lack of knowledge of actual trends in the locations of job opportunities, costs of urban infrastructure for "growth-pole" development, ignorance of the location requirements of different industries, and lack of understanding of migration principles. Laquian and Simmons conclude their review with a recommendation for integrated planning for migration control, which I interpret to mean a more complete consideration of structural or ecological factors.

Mention was made earlier of policies to control population distribution and industrial locations in centrally planned socialist and in developed neighboring countries (Fuchs and Demke 1979; Tabb and Sawers 1978, 338–43). In both settings the policies failed to realize their purposes and for very similar reasons. Neither took into account the limited degrees of freedom afforded by the existing transportation networks.

In much the same vein the United States government has sought to restore the attractions of the inner areas of declining cities with programs of urban renewal and neighborhood rehabilitation. Despite expenditures of huge amounts of money on large-scale efforts, deconcentration trends have continued unabated. The experience has led some observers to suggest that the role of policy should be to reconcile inertia with change. Thus it has been said: "The real challenge is to design policies that address the worst aspects of urban decline without radically assaulting long-entrenched institutional arrangements, that correct the workings of markets without trying to over-ride them wholesale," (Bradbury, Downs, and Small 1982, 296). How that is to be accomplished while modern facilities for transportation and communication continue to erode the values of proximity is not stated. Institutional entrenchment and market forces operate in a context set by the composition of mobility costs.

Policy addressed to an accommodation to change in process is manifested in the actions of many third world countries in giving official support to nationwide fertility control programs. The introduction of such policies followed the onset of fertility decline by as much as a decade. Belated though they were, the policies acknowledged the need to accelerate the rates of decline in order to shorten the period of excessive population growth.

Returning to the developed world, a recent policy proposal in the United States advocates an acceptance of urban deconcentration and recommends providing assistance for the movement of persons to places where industries are relocating (President's Commission for a National Agenda for the Eighties 1980). The proposal conforms to the ongoing trend. It says little, however, about what is to be done with the large capital accumulations represented in the physical installations of cities. Unrelated to the deconcentration proposal, though consistent with it, is the building of wholly planned suburban towns, complete with sets of consumer services, many with the aid of planning and construction subsidies from the federal government. A revealing study matched seventeen planned towns with an equal number of conventional towns on age, location, and housing types and price ranges, and compared the two samples with reference to residents' satisfaction, population turnover, racial mixing, and participation by residents in community life. The findings indicated that the planned communities did not differ appreciably from unplanned or conventional towns (Burby and Weiss 1976). Evidently the planning, though in accord with prevailing trends, could not manage to turn the trends in what were thought to be desirable directions.

Efforts to produce change through the implementation of policy may, when successful, produce side effects that cost as much as or more than the benefits gained. Official policies favoring the introduction of new high-yield varieties of rice in rice-producing countries of the third world converted some from rice-importing to rice-exporting countries. To that extent the policies were successful. But the capital requirements for irrigation and the tools needed for the cultivation of the new strains of rice necessitated increases in farm sizes. A result was the displacement of many small farmers from the land and substantial increases in unemployment (Brown 1970, 77–121). On the other hand, the increased productivity of rice lands brought prices down, and the cheaper rice overcame the strong preferences among consumers for the more familiar strains of rice. Adaptability of that kind is not uncommon. A willingness on the part of preliterate and peasant people, among whom the weight of tradition is assumed to be especially heavy, to forsake folk prejudices and values when superior opportunities or products are available has often been observed (Firth 1954; Jahoda 1962; Gugler 1969; Gerschenkron 1953).

None of the remarks here should be taken to imply that policy cannot be effective in producing or controlling change to obtain desired results. My point is rather that successful policies are those that give full consideration to the kinds of structural factors identified in the principles of human ecology. And here I agree with Murdock in his criticism of popularized "ecological principles," as represented in neo-Malthusianism and simple analogies from plant and animal ecology (1980, 310–13). My reference is to principles that govern the interactions among units of organization. As a first principle it should be recognized that cumulative increases in the efficiency of mobility tend toward a randomization of location values while raising the probabilities of change in all sectors of an ecosystem.

Nor is it my purpose to denigrate the political economy approach. Attention to the interactions among representatives of vested interests is unquestionably productive of understanding how changes come about or fail to come about in specific instances. It is a truism that the more particular or practical is the problem one attacks, the more necessary it is to draw upon the contributions of various disciplines. That is nowhere better illustrated, for example, than in the problem of disposing of pollution of the air and ocean. Knowledge from economics, political science, and engineering, as well as from human ecology, must be brought to bear on the problem. The same may be said of country-specific problems of development, industrial relocations, population distribution, and the like. Thus the political economy approach is appropriately titled. But that leaves unanswered the question of whether that approach can yield general knowledge about the interactions among factors involved in ecosystem development.

Notes

Chapter 1

1. An effort to counter this tendency has been put forward in a seminal essay by Siegel (1984). My present position on this matter differs considerably from what I held some years ago. Then (1944) I argued that human ecology erred in wandering too far from general ecology. I now believe that such a position is not entirely tenable; it needs to be modified by a respect for the exigencies of the human situation.

Chapter 2

1. It has been observed that bird niches in Chile and California are structured quite differently, although both locations have Mediterranean climates and other environmental similarities. Cody (1973) attributes the difference to historical accident.

2. Portugal is reported to have experienced so great an emigration to its colonies in the sixteenth century that it encountered severe labor shortages. Accordingly, its government imposed a ban on further emigration (Pierson 1942, 113).

3. In bioecology the ecosystem is usually defined to include the proximate environment to encompass the entire cycle of energy

flows. *Environment* in my usage is held apart from the ecosystem so that it may be treated as an independent variable.

4. This distinction has appeared in many guises in the sociological literature, as in Durkheim's (1933) distinction between organic and mechanic solidarity, Tönnies's (1957) contrast of *Gemeinshaft* with *Gesellschaft*, and Abel's (1935) and Coleman's (1975) classifications of relations on the basis of interest and sentiment.

5. The concept *niche*, though defined as a property of a system, is commonly operationalized as an occupation practiced by a category of units. Whether the occupation is dispensible relative to the continuity of the system suggests a test for its being a system property. I am not aware of the test having been applied.

6. A difference between these two primitive instances, assuming the descriptions offered are complete, is that the Shoshone occupied their habitat at the Malthusian limit while the !Kung lived well below the maximum carrying capacity of their habitat.

7. Courtland Smith (1980) has reported that wealth distributions in tribal societies approach the shape of a normal curve, whereas in peasant communities of state societies wealth distributions are more log normal.

8. A new measure for the standard meter, prepared by the National Bureau of Standards, is time, as represented in the speed of light, which is ten times more accurate than the formerly used wave length of optical radiation (Robinson 1983).

9. For a careful examination of physical, chemical, and biological uses of equilibrium, consult Bailey (1984).

Chapter 3

1. The critical importance, if not the primacy, of transportation and communication technology in all other technical advances has been suggested in a number of empirical studies. Olsen (1968) found that number of motor vehicles is the one factor consistently highly associated with indications of political development in a sample of nations. Again Nolan (1979) observed, in a study of seventy nations, that the numbers of telephones and motor vehicles per capita are closely associated with governmental size independent of population size and concentrations. Accessibility, says Lewis (1957, 53), plays a decisive part in stimulating economic growth.

2. In discussions of technological change, a distinction is often made between invention and innovation. The former is the synthesis of information to constitute a new element. The latter refers to applying an invention. The mechanical aspect of technology is most prominent in the invention component, although invention also pre-

supposes various support arrangements, such as families, schools, communication facilities, industries, patent offices, and others. The organizational element comes into fullest view at the innovation state, inasmuch as industries must be reorganized, capital assembled, and structural accommodations made throughout the system. Innovation also requires, of course, a dovetailing of the new invention with preexisting mechanical contrivances.

3. Duncan (1964) has so ably reviewed the ecological foundation of evolution that no improvement on his presentation can be offered here.

4. Geneticists have commented on the rate of evolution as affected by population size. The larger the population, the slower the rate is apt to be, for the proportion of mutant genes in the total gene content is small. Should a large population be broken into smaller aggregates, the proportion of mutant genes in each of the fragments becomes, or may become, relatively large. The pace of change may be quickened therefore (Haskins 1951:121–30).

5. Retention, following selection, is sometimes included as a third factor in the biological model (Campbell 1969). But it is not evident that retention adds anything that is essential to the model. If selection has occurred, the mutant form is retained; if the mutant form is not retained, selection has failed to occur.

6. Dunbar (1972) has forcefully argued that the ecosystem, not the individual or species, is the unit of natural selection. He notes that ecosystems reject species that threaten their adaptive stability. That observation, however, would seem to turn the argument in a different direction. That is, if rejected species may be regarded as elements of the ecosystem's environment, then it would seem that the ecosystem rather than the environment is the active selective agent.

7. A distinction has been drawn between specific and general evolution with reference to their effects for adaptability (Sahlins and Service 1960). Specific evolution, as represented in increased specialization, leads to a diminution or loss of adaptability. On the other hand, general evolution, defined as change toward suitability for the widest possible range of environments, results in a maximization of adaptability. Specific evolution, it is further said, is terminal, whereas general evolution tends to be continuous. From a system point of view, however, specialization of the individual or species, when joined with the specialties of other individuals or species, raises the adaptive capability of the system. Adaptation, to repeat a point made earlier, is a system process.

Chapter 4

1. A multivariate analysis of the adoption of agricultural innova-

tions in Indian villages demonstrated the significance of village leaders (Fliegel et al. 1968, 102).

2. This sequence of demographic changes has been described as the "demographic transition" (Notestein 1953). The transition is repeated wherever cumulative change is uninterrupted and unreversed, though the specific content of change may differ from place to place. In the Western world the transition followed revolutionary changes in production technology, whereas in areas in which changes in production technology have been much slower, an importation of Western mortality-control knowledge has had a similar effect (Coale 1973; Teitelbaum 1975). An important point in this connection is that fertility decline is contingent on a prior mortality decline. A seeming exception results from the dual effect of improvement in health conditions of reducing mortality and also allowing more pregnancies to terminate in live births (Habakkuk 1953).

3. This axiom has had a venerable lineage. D'Arcy Thompson, who applied the rule in his biological studies, attributes its first statement to Galileo (1963, 27). Herbert Spencer (1868, 2:281), however, anticipated Thompson by half a century in his awareness of the principle. The idea has been employed more recently by Mason Haire (1959, chap. 10) and by Kenneth Boulding (1953).

4. From his analysis of historical data pertaining to preindustrial England, Lee (1980, 546–47) concluded: "The economy could absorb population growth of about 0.4% per year with little effect; deviations of population size above or below this trend line, however, had dramatic consequences. And perhaps more striking than the existence of their effects is the extreme sensitivity of the economy's reaction; reckoning in terms of agricultural goods, a 10% increase in population depressed wages by 22%, raised rents by 19%, lowered industrial prices relative to agricultural prices by 17%, raised the ratio of industrial to agricultural production by 13%, and lowered labor's share of national income by 14%."

5. Friedrich (1978) provides us with a simple illustration of how market expansion affects differentiation. The enlarged market for craft products of medieval German cities could not be exploited without the emergence of a new class of specialists. Members of guilds who had capital for purchasing raw materials and the means for distributing products acquired an entrepreneurial role. Production became organized in what was to be known as the "putting out" system. Thus what had been a middle class of master craftsmen was soon divided into upper and lower middle classes, the latter once removed from direct market contact.

6. Norbert Elias (1982, 235–36) contends that civility in interpersonal relations is contingent on a centralization (i.e., monopolization) of power from which follows increases in divisions of functions, a

lengthening of chains of action binding individuals together, and a weakening of kinship as basis for allocating functions to population in a division of labor.

7. According to Richard Levins (1973, 113–14), "The general strategy for analyzing complex systems is through some decomposition into subsystems and their interactions. In engineering, where the parts are produced separately, retain their identity, and behave in the systems the way they behave outside it, the physical components themselves may be chosen as the 'natural' systems. Even here the choice may be misleading, but applied to evolved systems it is often disastrous. At any rate, we cannot accept these commonsense components as the best decomposition, nor can they be accepted as fixed in the context of evolution."

8. I have been unable to find any counterpart to vertical mobility in the literature on the biotic ecosystem.

9. Hardin (1960) has stated a principle of "competitive exclusion" to explain this kind of outcome. According to the principle, since two unlike populations cannot occupy a given niche, one must be excluded in the ensuing competition. The principle seems to express a redundancy, however, for unlike populations do not enter into competition for a given resource space.

10. It may, however, have what could be regarded as a "market," or an unassimilated clientele. That is, a mission orientation in a categoric unit, for example, a religious denomination, views the uncounted nonmembers as candidates for receiving the benefits of the unit. The process of proselytizing may be regarded as competitive response.

11. The *Encyclopedia of Associations* (1980) lists approximately eleven thousand regional, national, and international associations having central offices.

12. Aldrich and Pfeffer (1976) have noted a number of theoretical and operational problems with the evolution-selection model, including inadequacies of cross-sectional analysis, lack of organization taxonomy, identification of sources of change, risks of tautological reasoning, determination of environmental boundaries, and neglect of the bearing of internal changes in organizations on their probabilities of survival.

13. It has been observed that urban growth processes in the Soviet Union do not differ significantly from those in the capitalist countries of the West (Tabb and Sawers 1978, 338–43). Further, the authors of a careful review of population redistribution policies in socialist and nonsocialist countries find that such policies have been no more successful in the former than in the latter (Fuchs and Demke 1979). Alfred Meyer (1970) offers an excellent analysis of theories of convergence, pro and con, with special reference to socialist-nonsocialist comparisons.

14. In their analysis of technological change, Frisbie et al. (1984) demonstrated that, while the process of change accelerated in the 1950–70 period in all countries in a sample of sixty-six, the relative positions of the countries on a scale of technological development remained the same. Later Lenski and Nolan (1984) shed some light on the Frisbie et al. finding. In their study of a sample of seventy-seven countries they found that those with horticultural preindustrial economies followed a different trajectory in their industrialization process than did those that had agrarian preindustrial economies. They infer, therefore, that a prior system–biophysical environment relation persists as an independent influence in subsequent changes. The two studies suggest that an unqualified convergence hypothesis is an oversimplification.

Chapter 5

1. This point is extensively discussed in Hawley 1950, chap. 15.

2. See Hoover (1948) for an economic analysis of transportation costs.

3. McNeill (1963, 296) has shown that China and the Roman Empire were engaged in trade relations as early as the second century A.D. Such long, thin lines, however, could convey only high value, luxury goods that had little direct consequences for most of the populations.

4. According to Ringrose (1970, 133), the development of Castile, Spain, stagnated during the latter part of the eighteenth and early nineteenth centuries, owing to a reliance on cart and wagon transportation of food and other bulk goods. And that mode of long-distance carriage was possible only so long as lands along the routes were usable for grazing draught animals. Later, as lands were enclosed for cultivation, grazing privileges disappeared. Thereafter transportation became an acute problem.

5. "The development of long-distance trade," say Vasina, Thomas, and Thomas (1964, 85), "seems to have been related to political development. For while political centralization may not have been indispensable for trade to develop and flourish, the development of trade itself in some areas favored the creation of centralized political systems. And these in turn contributed in large measure to further development of trade by providing organization and security for markets and caravans. A close link between long-distance trade and state organization must then be assumed in many states." Braudel (1984, 72–88) finds evidence of a broad interregional, if not a world, system in the conjunctions of rhythms of grain price swings among widely separated places and in the rapid movements of economic information existing as early as the sixteenth century.

6. Exceptions have been noted. Murphey (1954) found that in Chinese cities under the empire, innovation seldom occurred. Bureaucratic rigidities and discouragement of trade were suggesed as the stultifying circumstances. Warner (1966) contends that in the American colonial period innovation took place in the countryside rather than in a metropolitan center.

7. Taffee, Merrill, and Gould (1963) have observed this sequence of steps in railroad development in Nigeria and Ghana, as did McKenzie (1927) before them in regard to the United States rail network.

8. Martin (1962) demonstrated a reasonably close relationship between amount of urbanization in a country and the spread of interregional trade relations (see also Gibbs and Martin 1958). A later study by Frisbie and Eberstein found a significant relation between functional differentiation and the extent of trade relations, with some variations by product type and size of place.

9. See my treatment of this aspect of urban pattern in Hawley 1978, chap. 5.

10. The gradient conforms to the expression $d_x = d_o e^{-bx}$, where d_x is density at distance x, d_o is density at the center, e is a natural logarithm, and b is the slope of density differences (Clark 1951; Duncan 1957).

11. Stephan and Tedrow (1977) examined the relation of city area size to population density, market potential, and travel time to and from the center. The finding was that travel time had the greatest explanatory power.

12. In a study of gasoline consumption changes in the 1960–70 decade in the United States, Zelinsky and Sly (1984) found that while substantial increases occurred in all of the metropolitan places, the smallest increases developed in the noncentral or ring counties. The authors concluded that deconcentration leads to fuel efficiency.

13. Ordinarily where minor civil divisions have some administrative autonomy, a majority vote in each approving an annexation to a larger administrative unit is required. That requirement is absent where there is not autonomy in outlying localities.

14. Polacek's (1980) study of international conflict showed the incidence of conflict to be highest where trade relations are weakest or nonexistent.

15. David Smith (1984) has arrived at a more elaborate stratification involving no less than four and possibly as many as eight strata.

16. Hymer (1975, 38) speaks of a "law of uneven development" that produces a hierarchical territorial division of labor, among regions, corresponding to the vertical division of labor within the firm. High-level decision making is concentrated in a few key cities surrounded by a number of regional subcapitals, with the rest of the world confined to low levels of activity and income. See also Chandler and Redlich 1961.

Chapter 6

1. Commenting on the S-curve of change in the past century, John Platt (1969) estimates, "we have increased our speed of communication by a factor of 10^7; our speed of travel by 10^2; our speed of data handling by 10^6; our energy resources by 10^3; our power of weapons by 10^6; our ability to control diseases by something like 10^2; our rate of population growth by 10^3 times what it was a few thousand years ago."

2. In 1958 Paul Sears (1958, 13) wrote: "My guess is that farm surpluses will be only a memory within two decades." A short while later Paul Ehrlich (1968, xi) declared: "The battle to feed humanity is over. In the 1970's the world will undergo famines—hundreds of millions of people are going to starve to death." Needless to say, these dire forecasts did not materialize.

3. A study of energy consumed per unit of crop land and value of crop sold demonstrated for the United States an inverse relation to farm size (Heaton and Brown 1982).

4. There are indications that food supplies in Europe prior to the nineteenth century were far more meager than those in contemporary developing countries (Teuteberg 1975; Fourastie 1951; Hale 1973). Gale Johnson (1974) reported that only one-tenth as many people died of starvation in the third quarter of the twentieth century as in the last quarter of the sixteenth century, despite the much larger population.

References

Abel, Theodore. 1935. "The Significance of the Concept of Consciousness of Kind." *Social Forces* 9:1–10.

Abramowitz, M. 1956. "Resources and Output in the United States since 1879." *American Economics Review* 46:5–23.

Adams, Robert McC. 1965. *The Evolution of Urban Society.* Chicago: Aldine.

Adelman, Irma, and Cynthia Morris. 1965. "A Factor Analysis of the Interrelationship between Social and Political Variables and Gross National Product." *Quarterly Journal of Economics* 79:555–78.

Aldrich, Howard, and Ellen R. Auster. 1986. "Even Dwarfs Started Small: Liabilities of Age and Size and Their Strategic Implications." In *Research in Organizational Behavior*, ed. Larry Cummings and Barry M. Staw. Greenwich, Conn.: JAI Press.

Aldrich, Howard, and Jeffrey Pfeffer. 1976. "Environments and Organizations." *Annual Review of Sociology* 2:79–105.

Anderson, Theodore R., and Seymour Warkov. 1961. "Organizational Size and Functional Complexity." *American Sociological Review* 26:23–28.

Arrow, Kenneth T. 1971. *Essays on the Theory of Risk Planning.* Chicago: University of Chicago Press.

Ashton, T. S. 1964. *The Industrial Revolution, 1760–1830.* New York: Oxford.

Bailey, Kenneth D. 1984. "Equilibrium, Entropy, and Homeostatis: A Multi-Disciplinary Legacy." *Systems Research* 1:25–43.

Baldridge, J. Victor, and Robert A. Burnham. 1975. "Organizational Innovations: Individual, Organizational, and Environmental Impacts." *Administrative Science Quarterly* 20:165–76

Barker, Roger G. 1960. "Ecology and Motivation." In *Nebraska Symposium on Motivation,* ed. Marshall R. Jones. Lincoln: University of Nebraska Press.

Barnett, H. J., and C. Morse. 1963. *Scarcity and Growth.* Baltimore: Johns Hopkins University Press.

Barnum, Howard N. 1976. "The Interrelationship among Social and Political Variables, Economic Structure, and Rural-Urban Migration." *Economic Development and Cultural Change* 24:759–64.

Bendix, Rinehardt. 1964. *Nation Building and Citizenship.* New York: Wiley.

Bennett, John W. 1976. *The Ecological Transition: Cultural Anthropology and Human Adaptation.* New York: Pergamon.

Benson, J. 1975. "Interorganizational Networks as a Political Economy." *Administrative Science Quarterly* 20:229–49.

Berry, Brian J. L. 1965. "Research Frontiers in Urban Geography." In *The Study of Urbanization,* ed. Philip M. Hauser and Leo F. Schnore. New York: Wiley.

Berry, Brian J. L., and John D. Kasarda. 1977. *Contemporary Urban Ecology.* New York: Macmillan.

Bertalanffy, Ludwig von. 1952. *Problems of Life: An Evaluation of Modern Biological and Scientific Thought.* New York: Harper.

Bidwell, Charles E., and John D. Kasarda. 1985. *The Organization and Its Ecosystem: A Theory of Structuring in Organizations.* Greenwich, Conn.: JAI Press.

Binford, Lewis R. 1968. "Post-Pleistocene Adaptations." In *New Perspectives in Archaeology,* ed. Sally R. Binford and Lewis Binford. Chicago: Aldine.

Blau, Peter. 1970. "A Formal Theory of Differentiation in Organizations." *American Sociological Review* 35:201–18.

Bollen, Kenneth. 1983. "World System Position, Dependency, and Democracy: The Cross-National Evidence." *American Sociological Review* 48:468–79.

Boserup, Ester. 1976. "Environment, Population, and Technology in Primitive Societies." *Population and Development Review* 2:21–36.

Boulding, Kenneth. 1934. "The Application of Pure Theory of Population Change to the Theory of Capital." *Quarterly Journal of Economics* 48:645–66.

———. 1953. "Toward a General Theory of Growth." *Canadian Journal of Economics and Political Science* 19:326–40.

———. 1969. "Technology and the Changing Social Order." In *The Urban-Industrial Frontier: Essays on Social Trends and Institutional Goals in Modern Communities*, ed. David Popenoe. New Brunswick, N.J.: Rutgers University Press.

———. 1975. "The Limits to Societal Growth." In *Societal Growth: Processes and Implications*, ed. Amos H. Hawley. New York: Free Press.

———. 1978. *Ecodynamics: A New Theory of Societal Evolution.* Beverly Hills, Calif.: Sage.

Bowen, Howard R., and Garth L. Mangum, eds. 1966. *Automation and Economic Progress.* Englewood Cliffs, N.J.: Prentice-Hall.

Bradbury, Katherine, Anthony Downs, and Kenneth A. Small. 1982. *Urban Decline and the Future of American Cities.* Washington, D.C.: Brookings Institution.

Braidwood, Robert A., and Gordon Willey, eds. 1962. *Courses toward Urban Life: Archaeological Considerations of Some Cultural Alternatives.* Chicago: Aldine.

Branscomb, Lewis M. 1979. "Information: The Ultimate Frontier." *Science* 203:143–47.

Braudel, Ferdinand. 1966. *The Mediterranean and the Mediterranean World in the Age of Philip II*, vol. 1. New York: Harper and Row.

———. 1984. *The Perspective of the World: Civilization and Capitalism, 15th–18th Centuries*, vol. 3. New York: Harper and Row.

Brittain, Jack W., and John Freeman. 1980. "Organizational Proliferation and Density Dependent Selection: Organizational Evolution in the Semi-Conductor Industry." In *Organizational Life Cycles*, ed. John Kimberly, John Miles, and Associates. San Francisco: Jossey-Bass.

Brooks, Harvey. 1980. "Technology, Evolution, and Purpose." *Daedalus* 109:65–81.

Brown, Lester. 1970. *Seeds of Change: The Green Revolution and Development in the 1970's.* New York: Praeger.

Buckley, Walter. 1967. *Sociology and Modern Systems Theory*. Englewood Cliffs, N.J.: Prentice-Hall.

Buer, Mabel. 1926. *Health, Wealth, and Population in the Early Days of the Industrial Revolution*. London: Routledge.

Burby, Raymond J., and Shirley F. Weiss. 1976. *New Communities. U.S.A.* Lexington, Mass.: Heath.

Burgess, Earnest W. 1925. "The Growth of the City: An Introduction to a Research Project." In *The City*, ed. Robert E. Park, Earnest W. Burgess, and Roderick D. McKenzie. Chicago: University of Chicago Press.

Buschbaum, Ralph, and Mildred Buschbaum. 1957. *Basic Ecology*. Pittsburgh: Boxwood Press.

Cain, Stanley. 1960. "Some Principles of General Ecology and Human Ecology." *American Biology Teacher* 22:60–164.

Campbell, D. T. 1969. "Variation and Selective Retention in Socio-Cultural Evolution." *General Systems* 14:69–85.

Carlsson, G. 1968. "Change, Growth, and Irreversibility." *American Journal of Sociology* 73:706–14.

Carniero, R. L. 1967. "On the Relationship between the Size of Population and Complexity of Social Organization." *Southwestern Journal of Anthropology* 23:234–42.

———. 1970. "A Theory of the Origin of the State." *Science* 169:733–38.

Carniero, R. L., and S. F. Tobias. 1963. "The Application of Scale Analysis to the Study of Evolution." *Transactions of the New York Academy of Science*, series 2, 26:196–207.

Carroll, Glenn R. 1984. "Organizational Ecology." *Annual Review of Sociology* 10:71–93.

Chandler, Alfred D. 1977. *The Visible Hand: The Managerial Revolution in American Business*. Cambridge: Harvard University Press.

Chandler, Alfred D., and F. Redlich. 1961. "Recent Developments in American Business Administration and Their Conceptualizations." *Business History Review* 35:1–27.

Chase-Dunn, Christopher. 1975. "The Effects of International Economic Dependence on Development and Inequality: A Cross-National Study." *American Sociological Review* 40:720–38.

Clark, Colin. 1951. "Urban Population Densities." *Journal of the Royal Statistical Society* 114:490–96.

Clemente, Frank, and Richard A. Sturgis. 1978. "The Division of Labor in America: An Ecological Analysis." *Social Forces* 51:176–82.

Clements, Frederic. 1916. *Plant Succession: An Analysis of the Development of Vegetation.* Washington, D.C.: Carnegie Institute.

Clements, Frederic, and V. E. Shelford. 1939. *Bioecology.* New York: Wiley.

Coale, Ansley. 1973. "The Demographic Transition Reconsidered." In *Papers Presented to the International Population Conference,* Liege.

Cochran, Thomas. 1968. "The Business Revolution." *American Historical Review* 79:14–50.

Cody, M. L. 1973. "Parallel Evolution and Bird Niches." In *Mediterranean Type Ecosystems,* Ecological Studies 7, ed. F. diCastro and H. A. Mooney. New York: Springer-Verlag.

Cohen, Mark. 1977. *The Food Crisis in Prehistory: Overpopulation and the Origin of Agriculture.* New Haven: Yale University Press.

Cole, Arther H. 1968. "The Entrepreneur: Introductory Remarks." *American Economics Review* 58:61–62.

Coleman, James. 1975. "Social Structure and a Theory of Action." In *Approaches to the Study of Social Structure,* ed. Peter M. Blau. New York: Free Press.

———. 1979. "The Measurement of Societal Growth." In *Societal Growth: Processes and Implications,* ed. Amos H. Hawley. New York: Free Press.

Cooley, Charles H. 1930. "Theory of Transportation." In *Sociological Theory and Social Research,* ed. Robert C. Angell. New York: Holt, Rinehart, and Winston.

Craven, P., and B. Wellman. 1973. "The Network City." *Sociological Inquiry* 43:57–88.

Davis, Kingsley, and Wilbert E. Moore. 1945. "Some Principles of Stratification." *American Sociological Review* 10:243–49.

Dewey, John. 1925. *Experience and Nature.* New York: W. W. Norton.

Dice, Lee. 1952. *Natural Communities.* Ann Arbor: University of Michigan Press.

Dos Santos, T. 1973. "The Crisis of Development Theory and the Problem of Dependence in Latin America." In *Underdevelopment and Development,* ed. H. Bernstein. Hammondsworth: Penguin.

Dumond, Don E. 1975. "The Limitation of Human Population: A Natural History." *Science* 187:713–21.

Dunbar, M. J. 1972. "The Ecosystem as a Unit of Natural Selection." *Transactions of the Connecticut Academy of Arts and Sciences* 44:113–30.

Duncan, Otis D. 1957a. "Optimum Sizes of Cities." In *Cities and Society*, ed. Paul K. Hatt and Albert J. Reiss, Jr. New York: Free Press.

————. 1957b. "Population Distribution and Community Structure." In *Cold Spring Harbor Symposium on Quantitative Biology: Population Studies: Animal Ecology and Demography.* Cold Spring Harbor, N.Y.: Biological Laboratory.

————. 1964. "Social Organization and the Ecosystem." In *Handbook of Modern Sociology*, ed. R. E. L. Faris. Chicago: Rand-McNally.

Duncan, Otis D., and Albert J. Reiss, Jr. 1956. *Social Characteristics of Urban and Rural Communities, 1950*. New York: Wiley.

Duncan, Otis D., W. Richard Scott, Stan Leiberson, Beverly Duncan, and Hal H. Winsborough. 1960. *Metropolis and Region*. Baltimore: Johns Hopkins University Press.

Durkheim, Emil. 1933. *The Division of Labor in Society*, trans. George Simpson. New York: Macmillan.

Eberstein, Isaac W., and Parker Frisbie. 1982. "Metropolitan Function and Interdependence in the U.S. Urban System." *Social Forces* 60:676–700.

Ehrlich, Paul. 1968. *The Population Bomb*. New York: Ballantine.

Elias, Norbert. 1982. *Power and Civility: The Civilizing Process*, vol. 2. New York: Pantheon.

Elvin, Mark. 1973. *The Pattern of the Chinese Past*. Stanford, Calif.: Stanford University Press.

Emmel, Thomas. 1973. *An Introduction to Ecology and Population Biology*. New York: W. W. Norton.

Encyclopedia of Associations. 1980. Detroit: Gale Publishing Co.

Evans, Peter, and Michael Timberlake. 1980. "Dependence, Inequality, and Growth in Less Developed Countries." *American Sociological Review* 45:531–52.

Feller, I. 1971. "The Urban Location of United States Inventions, 1800–1910." *Explorations in Economic History* 8:285–303.

Ferdon, Edwin. 1959. "Agricultural Potential and the Development of Cultures." *Southwestern Journal of Anthropology* 15:1–19.

Firth, Raymond. 1954. "Money, Work, and Social Change in Indo-Pacific Economic Systems." *International Social Science Bulletin* 6:400–411.

Fisher, F. J. 1971. "London as an Engine of Economic Growth." In *Britain and the Netherlands IV*, ed. J. S. Bromley and E. H. Kossman. The Hague: Martinus Nijhoff.

Fliegel, Frederick C., Prodipto Roy, Latit K. Sen, and Joseph E. Kivlin. 1968. *Agricultural Innovations in Indian Villages.* Hyderabad: National Institute of Community Development.

Fourastie, Jean. 1951. *The Causes of Wealth*, trans. Theodore Caplow. New York: Free Press.

Freeman, Linton C., and Robert F. Winch. 1957. "Societal Complexity: An Empirical Test of a Typology of Societies." *American Journal of Sociology* 62:461–66.

Friedrich, C. J., ed. 1929. *Alfred Weber's Theory of the Location of Industries.* Chicago: University of Chicago Press.

Friedrich, Christopher. 1978. "Capitalism, Mobility, and Class Formation in the Medieval German City." In *Towns in Societies: Essays in Economic History and Historical Sociology*, ed. Philip Abrams and E. A. Wrigley. Cambridge: Cambridge University Press.

Frisbie, Parker, and Clifford Clark. 1979. "Technology in Evolutionary and Ecological Perspective: Theory and Measurement at the Societal Level," *Social Forces* 58:591–613.

Frisbie, Parker, Lauren J. Krive, Robert L. Kaufman, Clifford J. Clark, and David E. Myers. 1984. "A Measurement of Technological Change: An Ecological Perspective." *Social Forces* 62:750–66.

Fuchs, Roland J., and George J. Demke. 1979. "Population Distribution Policies in Developed Socialist Countries and Western Nations." *Population and Development Review* 5:439–68.

Galaskiewicz, Joseph. 1979. "The Structure of Community Organization Networks." *Social Forces* 57:1346–64.

Galle, Omar. 1963. "Occupational Composition and the Metropolitan Hierarchy: the Inter- and Intrametropolitan Division of Labor." *American Journal of Sociology* 69:260–69.

Gerschenkron, Alexander. 1953. "Social Attitudes, Entrepreneurship, and Economic Development." *Explorations in Entrepreneurial History* 6:1–15.

Gibbs, Jack P., and Walter T. Martin. 1958. "Urbanization and

Natural Resources: A Study in Organizational Ecology." *American Sociological Review* 23:266–77.

Goeller, H. E., and A. M. Weinberg. 1976. "The Age of Substitutability." *Science* 191:683–89.

Goldschmidt. Walter. 1959. *Man's Way: A Preface to an Understanding of Human Society.* New York: Holt, Rinehart, and Winston.

Goodrich, Carter, Bushrod W. Allin, and C. Warren Thornwaite. 1936. *Migration and Economic Opportunity.* Philadelphia: University of Pennsylvania Press.

Gottfried, Robert S. 1983. *The Black Death: Natural and Human Disaster in Medieval Europe.* New York: Free Press.

Gould, Philip W. 1976. "Discovery of Natural Resources." *Science* 191:709–13.

Greer, Scott. 1979. "Discontinuities and Fragmentation in Societal Growth." In *Societal Growth: Processes and Implications*, ed. Amos H. Hawley. New York: Free Press.

Guest, Avery. 1969. "The Applicability of the Burgess Zonal Hypothesis to Urban Canada." *Demography* 6:271–77.

———. 1972. "Patterns of Family Location." *Demography* 9:159–72.

Gugler, Joseph. 1969. "On the Theory of Rural-Urban Migration: The Case of Subsaharan Africa." In *Migration*, ed. J. A. Jackson. Cambridge: Cambridge University Press.

Habakkuk, M. J. 1953. "English Population in the Eighteenth Century." *Economic History Review*, series 2, 6:117–33.

Haggerty, L. J. 1971. "Another Look at the Burgess Hypothesis: Time as an Important Variable." *American Journal of Sociology* 76:1084–93.

Haire, Mason. 1959. "Biological Models and Empirical Histories of the Growth of Organizations." In *Modern Organization Theory*, ed. Mason Haire. New York: Wiley.

Hale, J. R. 1973. *Renaissance Europe: The Individual and Society, 1480–1520.* New York: Harper and Row.

Hannan, Michael, and John Freeman. 1977. "The Population Ecology of Organizations." *American Journal of Sociology* 82:929–64.

———. 1984. "Structural Inertia and Organizational Change." *American Sociological Review* 49:149–64.

Hardin, Garret. 1960. "The Competitive Exclusion Principle." *Science* 133:1291–97.

——. 1968. "The Tragedy of the Commons," *Science* 162:1243–48.

Harris, Marvin. 1979. *Cultural Materialism: The Struggle for a Science of Culture.* New York: Random House.

Haskins, Caryl P. 1951. *Of Societies and Men.* New York: W. W. Norton.

Hawkes, R. K. 1973. "Spatial Patterning of Urban Population." *American Journal of Sociology* 78:1216–35.

Hawley, Amos H. 1944. "Ecology and Human Ecology." *Social Forces* 22:398–405.

——. 1950. *Human Ecology: A Theory of Community Structure.* New York: Ronald.

——. 1963. "Community Power and Urban Renewal Success." *American Journal of Sociology* 68:422–31.

——. 1969. "Population and Society: An Essay on Growth" In *Fertility and Family Planning: A World View*, ed. S. J. Behrman, Leslie Corsa, and Ronald Freedman. Ann Arbor: University of Michigan Press.

——. 1978. *Urban Society: An Ecological Approach.* New York: Wiley.

Heaton, Tim, and David L. Brown. 1982. "Farm Structure and Energy Intensity." *Rural Sociology* 47:17–31.

Higgs, Robert. 1975. "Urbanization and Inventiveness in the United States, 1870–1920." In *The New Urban History*, ed. Leo F. Schnore. Princeton: Princeton University Press.

Hirsch, Fred. 1976. *Social Limits to Growth.* Cambridge: Harvard University Press.

Hirschman, Albert O. 1958. *The Strategy of Economic Development.* New Haven: Yale University Press.

Hoover, E. M. 1948. *The Location of Economic Activity.* New York: McGraw-Hill.

Hoover, E. M., and Raymond Vernon. 1959. *Anatomy of A Metropolis: The Changing Distribution of People and Jobs within the New York Metropolitan Region.* Cambridge: Harvard University Press.

Hunter, Alfred. 1971. "The Ecology of Chicago: Persistence and Change." *American Journal of Sociology* 71:925–44.

Hymer, S. 1975. "The Multinational Corporation and the Law of Uneven Development." In *International Firms and Modern Imperialism.* Harmondsworth: Penguin.

Jahoda, Gustave. 1962. "Aspects of Modernization: A Study of

Adult-Class Students in Ghana." *British Journal of Sociology* 13:43–56.

Janowitz, Morris. 1952. *The Community Press in an Urban Setting.* Glencoe, Ill.: Free Press.

Johnson, D. Gale. 1974. Population, Food, and Economic Adjustment." *American Statistician* 28:89–93.

Kanter, Jeffrey. 1981. "Structural Determinants of Peripheral Urbanization: The Effects of International Dependence." *American Sociological Review* 46:201–11.

Karsh, Bernard, and Robert E. Cole. 1968. "Industrialization and the Convergence Hypothesis: Some Aspects of Contemporary Japan." *Journal of Social Issues* 24:45–64.

Kasarda, John D. 1974. "The Structural Implications of Social System Size: A Three-Level Analysis." *American Sociological Review* 39:19–28.

Kass, Roy. 1977. "Community Structure and the Metropolitan Division of Labor: The Impact of Key Functions on Community Social Characteristics." *Social Forces* 56:218–39.

Kendrick, John W. 1961. *Productivity Trends in the United States.* Princeton: Princeton University Press.

———. 1973. *Postwar Productivity Trends in the United States, 1948–1969.* New York: National Bureau of Economic Research.

Kirk, Dudley. 1971. "A New Demographic Transition." In *Rapid Population Growth: Consequences and Policy Implications.* Washington, D.C.: National Academy of Sciences.

Kroeber, A. L. 1939. *Cultural and Natural Areas of Native North America.* Berkeley: University of California Press.

Kuznets, Simon, 1978. "Technological Innovations and Economic Growth," In *Technological Innovation: A Critical Review of Knowledge,* ed. Patrick Kelly and Melvin Kranzburg. San Francisco: San Francisco Press.

Lambert, Richard D. 1964. "Some Consequences of Segmentation in India." *Economic Development and Cultural Change* 12:416–24.

Landsberg, H. H. 1976. "Materials: Some Recent Trends and Issues." *Science* 191:637–40.

Laquian, Aprodicio A., and Alan B. Simmons. 1979. "Public Policy and Migratory Behavior in Selected Cities." In *The Urban Impact of Migration,* ed. James W. White. Chapel Hill, N.C.: Institute for Research in Social Science.

Laumann, Edward D., Joseph Galaskiewicz, and Peter Marsden. 1978. "Community Structure and Organizational Linkages." In *Annual Review of Sociology* (Palo Alto: Annual Reviews, Inc.), vol. 4.

Lee, Richard B. 1979. *The Kung Sun: Men, Women, and Work in a Foraging Society.* Cambridge: Cambridge University Press.

Lee, Ronald D. 1980. "A Historical Perspective on Economic Aspects of the Population Explosion: The Case of Preindustrial England." In *Population and Economic Change in Developing Countries,* ed. Richard Easterlin. Chicago: University of Chicago Press.

Lenski, Gerhard, and Jean Lenski. 1982. *Human Societies: An Introduction to Macrosociology.* New York: McGraw-Hill.

Lenski, Gerhard, and Patrick D. Nolan. 1984. "Trajectories of Development: A Test of Ecological Evolutionary Theory." *Social Forces* 63:1–23.

Lesser, Alexander. 1961. "Social Fields and the Evolution of Society." *Southwestern Journal of Anthropology* 17:40–48.

Levins, Richard. 1973. "The Limits of Complexity." In *Hierarchic Theory: The Challenge of Complex Systems,* ed. Howard H. Pattee. New York: Braziller.

Levy, Marion J. 1952. *The Structure of Society.* Princeton: Princeton University Press.

Lewis, Arthur. 1957. *The Theory of Economic Growth.* London: Allen and Unwin.

Ley, Colin. 1982. "African Economic Development in Theory and Practice." *Daedalus,* spring, 99–124.

Lincoln, James R. 1976. "Power and Mobilization in the Urban Community: Reconsidering the Ecological Approach." *American Sociological Review* 41:1–15.

———. 1979. "Organizational Differentiation in Urban Communities: A Study in Organizational Ecology." *Social Forces* 57:915–30.

Lincoln, James R., and Roger Friedland. 1976. "Metropolitan Dominance and Income Levels in Nonmetropolitan Cities." *Sociology and Social Research* 61:304–19.

Logan, John R. 1976. "Industrialization and the Stratification of Cities in Suburban Regions." *American Journal of Sociology* 82:333–48.

Long, Clarence D. 1958. *The Labor Force under Changing Income and Employment.* Princeton: Princeton University Press.

Lotka, A. J. 1924. "The Statistical Meaning of Irreversibility." *Elements of Physical Biology.* Baltimore: Wilkins and Wilkins.

McKenzie, Roderick D. 1924. "The Ecological Approach to the Study of the Human Community." *American Journal of Sociology* 30:287–301.

———. 1926. "The Scope of Human Ecology." *American Journal of Sociology* 32:141–54.

———. 1927. "The Concept of Dominance and World Organization." *American Journal of Sociology* 33:28–42.

McNeill, William. 1963. *The Rise of the West*. Chicago: University of Chicago Press.

McPherson, Miller. 1983. "The Size of Voluntary Organizations." *Social Forces* 61:1044–64.

Malinowski, Bronislaw. 1938. "Culture." In *Encyclopedia of the Social Sciences*. New York: Macmillan.

Malthus, Thomas. 1914. *Essay on the Principle of Population*. London: Everyman.

Mantoux, Paul. 1927. *The Industrial Revolution in the Eighteenth Century*. New York: Harcourt, Brace.

Margalef, Ramon. 1968. *Perspectives in Ecological Theory*. Chicago: University of Chicago Press.

Mark, Harold, and Kent P. Schwirian. 1967. "Ecological Position, Urban Central Place Functions, and Community Population Growth." *American Journal of Sociology* 73:30–41.

Martin, Walter T. 1962. "Urbanization and National Power to Requisition Resources." *Pacific Sociological Review* 5:93–97.

Marx, Karl. 1904. *A Contribution to the Critique of Political Economy*. Chicago: Kerr.

———. 1936. *Capital*. Trans. by Samuel Moore and Edward Aveling. New York: Modern Library.

———. 1967. *Capital: A Critique of Political Economy*. ed. Frederick Engels. 3 vols. New York: International Publishers.

Masering, Catherine. 1976. "Factors Affecting the Carrying Capacity of Nation States." *Journal of Anthropological Research* 32:255–75.

Mayhew, Bruce H., and E. L. Levinger. 1976. "Size and Density of Interaction in Human Aggregates," *American Journal of Sociology* 82:86–110.

Mayhew, Bruce H., Robert L. Levinger, J. Miller McPherson, and Thomas F. James. 1972. "System Size and Structural Differentiation in Formal Organizations: A Baseline Generator for Two Major Theoretical Propositions." *American Sociological Review* 37:629–33.

Meadows, Donell H., Dennis L. Meadows, Jorgan Randers and William W. Behrens III. 1972. *The Limits to Growth*. New York: Universe.

Meggars, Betty J. 1954. "Environmental Limitations on the Development of Culture." *American Anthropologist* 56:801–24.

———. 1957. "Environment and Culture in the Amazon Basin: An Appraisal of the Theory of Environmental Determinism." In *Studies in Human Ecology*, pp. 71–90. Pan American Union: Washington, D.C.

Melbin, Murray. 1978. "Night as Frontier." *American Sociological Review* 43:3–22.

Meyer, Alfred. 1970. "Theories of Convergence." In *Change in Communist Systems*, ed. Chalmers Johnson. Stanford: Stanford University Press.

Meyer, John W., John Boli-Bennett, and Christopher Chase-Dunn. 1975. "Convergence and Divergence in Development." In *Annual Review of Sociology*, vol. 1. Palo Alto, Calif. Annual Reviews, Inc.

Mishan, E. J. 1977. *The Economic Growth Debate: An Assessment*. London: Allen and Unwin.

Moore, Wilbert E. 1963. *Social Change*. Englewood Cliffs, N.J.: Prentice-Hall.

———. 1979. *World Modernization: The Limits of Convergence*. New York: Elsevier.

Morgan, Lewis H. 1877. *Ancient Society*. Chicago: Kerr.

Morison, Robert S., ed. 1978. "Limits of Scientific Enquiry." *Daedalus*, spring.

Morrison, Peter A., and Allan Abrahamse. 1982. *Is Population Decentralization Lengthening Commuting Distances?* Santa Monica, Calif.: Rand Corporation.

Murdock, William W. 1980. *The Poverty of Nations: The Political Economy of Hunger and Population*. Baltimore: Johns Hopkins University Press.

Murphey, Rhoades. 1954. "The City as a Center of Change." *Annals of American Geographers* 44:347–62.

Naroll, Raoul. 1956. "A Preliminary Index of Social Development." *American Anthropologist* 58:687–716.

Nisbet, Robert A. 1969. *Social Change and History*. New York: Oxford University Press.

Nolan, Patrick D. 1979. "Area Distance, Contact Technology,

and Administrative Intensity in Societies." *Social Forces* 58:164–69.

Notestein, Frank W. 1953. "Economics of Population and Food Supplies: Economic Problems of Population Change." In *Proceedings of Eighth Annual Conference on Agricultural Economics*. London: Oxford University Press.

Odum, Eugene. 1969. "The Strategy of Ecosystem Development." *Science* 164:262–63.

Ogburn, W. F., and Otis D. Duncan. 1964. "City Size as a Sociological Variable." In *Contributions to Urban Sociology*, ed. Earnest W. Burgess and Donald J. Bogue. Chicago: University of Chicago Press.

Olsen, Marvin. 1968. "A Multivariate Analysis of National Political Development." *American Sociological Review* 33:699–712.

Olson, Mancur. 1982. *The Rise and Decline of Nations: Economic Growth, Stagflation, and Social Rigidities*. New Haven: Yale University Press.

Pappenfort, Donnell. 1959. "The Ecological Field and the Metropolitan Community: Manufacturing and Management." *American Journal of Sociology* 44:380–85.

Park, Robert E. 1925. "The Urban Community as a Spatial Pattern and a Moral Order." *Publications of the American Sociological Society* 20:1–14.

———. 1929. "Sociology, Community and Society." In *Research in the Social Sciences*, ed. Wilson Gee. New York: Macmillan.

———. 1936a. "Human Ecology." *American Journal of Sociology* 42:3–49.

———. 1936b. "Succession: An Ecological Concept." *American Sociological Review* 1:171–79.

Park, Robert E., and Earnest W. Burgess. 1921. *Introduction to the Science of Sociology*. Chicago: University of Chicago Press.

Parsons, Talcott. 1949. *The Structure of Social Action*. Glencoe, Ill.: Free Press.

———. 1951. *The Social System*. Glencoe, Ill.: Free Press.

———. 1961. *Theories of Society*. New York: Free Press.

Pearl, Raymond. 1930. *The Biology of Population Growth*. New York: Knopf.

Pennings, Johannes M. 1982. "Organizational Birth Frequencies: An Empirical Investigation." *Administrative Science Quarterly* 27:120–44.

Phythian-Adams, Charles. 1978. "Urban Decay in Late Medieval England." In *Towns in Societies*, ed. Philip Abrams and E. A. Wrigley. Cambridge: Cambridge University Press.

Pickett, S. T. A. 1976. "Succession: An Evolutionary Interpretation." *American Naturalist* 110:107–18.

Pierson, Donald. 1942. *Negroes in Brazil*. Chicago: University of Chicago Press.

Platt, John. 1969. "What We Must Do." *Science* 166:1115–21.

Polacek, Solomon W. 1980. "Conflict and Trade," *Journal of Conflict Resolution* 24:55–78.

Pondy, Louis R. 1969. "The Effects of Size, Complexity, and Ownership on Administrative Intensity." *Administrative Science Quarterly* 14:47–60.

Portes, Alejandro. 1979. "The Informal Sector and the World Economy: On the Structure of Subsidized Labor." *Institute for Development Studies Bulletin* 9:35–40.

Pred, Allan R. 1966. *The Spatial Dynamics of U.S. Urban-Industrial Growth, 1800–1914: Interpretive and Theoretical Essays*. Cambridge: MIT Press.

President's Commission for a National Agenda for the Eighties. 1980. *Urban America in the Eighties*. Washington, D.C.: Government Printing Office.

Quigley, Carroll. 1961. *The Evolution of Civilizations: An Introduction to Historical Analysis*. New York: Macmillan.

Ratzel, Friedrich. 1882–91. *Anthropogeographie*. Stuttgart: J. Engelhorns.

Ravelle, Roger. 1976. "The Resources Available for Agriculture." *Science* 235:164–79.

Redfield, Robert, and Milton Singer. 1954. "The Cultural Role of Cities." *Economic Development and Cultural Change* 3:53–71.

Ringrose, David R. 1970. *Transportation and Economic Stagnation in Spain, 1750–1850*. Durham, N.C.: Duke University Press.

Roberts, Bryan. 1978. *Cities of Peasants: The Political Economy of Urbanization in the Third World*. Beverly Hills, Calif.: Sage.

Robinson, Arthur L. 1983. "Using Time to Measure Length." *Science* 220:1367.

Robinson, E. A. G., ed. 1963. *Economic Consequences of the Size of Nations*. London: Macmillan.

Ross, Christopher. 1982. "Regional Patterns of Organizational Change. 1955–1975." *American Sociological Review* 23:207–19.

Rostow, Walt. 1960. *The Stages of Economic Growth*. New York: Cambridge University Press.

Rubinson, Richard. 1976. "The World Economy and the Distribution of Income within States: A Cross-National Study." *American Sociological Review* 41:638–59.

Rushing, William A. 1967. "The Effects of Industry Size and Division of Labor on Administration." *Administrative Science Quarterly* 12:273–95.

Ryder, Norman B. 1961. "Cohort Analysis." In *International Encyclopedia of the Social Sciences*. New York: Macmillan.

———. 1964 "Note on the Concept of Population." *American Journal of Sociology* 69:460–63.

———. 1965. "The Cohort as a Concept in the Study of Social Change." *American Sociological Review* 30:843–61.

Sahlins, Marshall. 1958. *Social Stratification in Polynesia*. Seattle: University of Washington Press.

Sahlins, Marshall, and Elman R. Service. 1960. *Evolution and Culture*. Ann Arbor: University of Michigan Press.

Sanders, William T., and Barbara Price. 1968. *Mesoamerica: The Evolution of Civilization*. New York: Random House.

Saunders, John V. D., and R. Rinehart. 1967. "Demographic and Economic Correlates of Development as Measured by Energy Consumption." *Demography* 4:773–79.

Sawyer, Jack. 1967. "Dimensions of Nations: Size, Wealth, and Politics." *American Journal of Sociology* 73:145–72.

Schnore, Leo F. 1957. "Satellites and Suburbs." *Social Forces* 36:121–27.

———. 1963. "The Social and Economic Characteristics of American Suburbs." *Sociological Quarterly* 4:122–34.

Schwartz, Richard D., and James C. Miller. 1964. "Legal Evolution and Societal Complexity." *American Journal of Sociology* 70:159–69.

Sears, Paul. 1958. "The Inexorable Problem of Space." *Science* 127:9–16.

Segal, David. 1976. "Are There Returns to Scale in City Size?" *Review of Economics and Statistics* 58:339–50.

Semple, Ellen C. 1911. *Influence of the Geographic Environment*. New York: Holt.

Siegel, Paul. 1984. "Human Ecology and Ecology." In *Sociological Human Ecology: Contemporary Issues and Applications*, ed. Michael Micklin and Harvey Choldin. Boulder, Colo.: Westview.

Simmons, Alan B. 1979. "Slowing Metropolitan Growth in Asia: Policies, Programs, and Results." *Population and Development Review* 5:87–104.

Simon, Herbert. 1962. "The Architecture of Complexity." *Proceedings of the American Philosophical Society* 106:467–82.

Simon, Julian. 1980. "Resources, Population, and Environment: An Oversupply of Fake Bad News." *Science* 208:1431–37.

Sjoberg, Gideon. 1960. *The Preindustrial City: Past and Present*. Glencoe, Ill.: Free Press.

Skinner, Reinhard J. 1976. "Technological Determinism: A Critique of Convergence Theory." *Comparative Studies in Society and History* 18:2–27.

Slobodkin, Lawrence B. 1962. *Growth and Regulation of Animal Populations*. New York: Holt, Rinehart, and Winston.

Smelser, Neil. 1959. *Social Change in the Industrial Revolution*. Chicago: University of Chicago Press.

Smith, Adam. 1937. *An Essay on the Nature and Causes of the Wealth of Nations*. New York: Modern Library.

Smith, Courtland L. 1980. Community Wealth Distribution: Comparisons in General Evolution and Development." *Economic Development and Cultural Change* 28:801–18.

Smith, David. 1984. *Urbanization in the World System: A Quantitative and Historical Structure Analysis*. Ph.D. diss., University of North Carolina.

Solow, Robert W. 1957. "Technical Change and the Aggregate Production Function." *Review of Economics and Statistics* 39:312–20.

Sorokin, Pitirim. 1941. *Social and Cultural Dynamics*, vol. 4. New York: Bedminster Press.

———. 1947. *Society, Culture, and Personality*. New York: Harper.

Spencer, Herbert. 1868. *The Principles of Sociology*, vol. 2. New York: Appleton.

Spencer, Robert J. 1959. *The North Alaskan Eskimo: A Study in Ecology and Society*. Bureau of American Ethnology, Bulletin 171. Washington, D.C.: Smithsonian Institution.

Steinhart, John S., and Carol Steinhart. 1974. "Energy Used in the U.S. Food System." *Science* 184:307–16.

Stephan, G. Edward, and Lucky M. Tedrow. 1977. "A Theory of Time-Minimization: The Relation between Urban Area and Population." *Pacific Sociological Review* 20:105–29.

Stevenson, Robert F. 1968. *Population and Political Systems in Tropical Africa*. New York: Columbia University Press.

Steward, Julian. 1938. *Basin-Plateau Aboriginal Sociopolitical Groups*. Bureau of American Ethnology, Bulletin 120. Washington, D.C.: Smithsonian Institution.

———. 1955. "Introduction." In *Irrigation Civilizations: A Comparative Study*. A Symposium on Method and Result in Cross-Cultural Regularities. Pan-American Union: Washington, D.C.

Stigler, G. T. 1957. "The Division of Labor is Limited by the Extent of the Market." *Journal of Political Economy* 59:187–91.

Stokinger, H. E. 1971. "Sanity in Research and Evaluation of Environmental Health." *Science* 174:662–65.

Strong, Donald, R., Jr., Daniel Simberloff, Lawrence C. Abele, and Anne B. Thistle, eds. 1984. *Ecological Communities: Conceptual Issues and the Evidence*. Princeton: University of Princeton Press.

Swanson, Guy E. 1971. *Social Change*. Glenview, Ill.: Scott Foresman.

Tabb, William K., and Larry Sawers, eds. 1978. *Marxism and the Metropolis: New Perspectives in Urban Political Economy*. New York: Oxford University Press.

Taffee, E. J., R. L. Merrill, and P. F. Gould. 1963. "Transportation Expansion in Underdeveloped Countries: A Comparative Analysis." *Geographical Review* 53:503–29.

Teitelbaum, Michael S. 1975. "The Relevance of Demographic Transition Theory for Developing Countries." *Science* 188:420–25.

Thompson, D'Arcy. 1962. *On Growth and Form*. Cambridge: Cambridge University Press.

Thompson, Wilber. 1962. "Locational Differences in Inventive Efforts and Their Determinants." In *The Rate and Direction of Inventive Activity: Economic and Social Factors*, National Bureau of Economic Research. Princeton: Princeton University Press.

Thunen, J. H. von. 1966. *The Isolated State*, trans. Carla Wartenbert. New York: Pergamon.

Tönnies, Ferdinand. 1957. *Community and Society: Gemeinschaft and Gesellschaft*, trans. Charles Loomis. New York: Harper and Row.

Toynbee, Arnold. 1956. *The Industrial Revolution*. Boston: Beacon.

Teuteberg, H. J. 1975. "The General Relationship between Diet and Industrialization." In *European Diet from Preindustrial to Modern Times*, ed. Elborg Forster and Robert Forster. New York: Harper and Row.

Turner, Ralph. 1940. "The Industrial City: Center of Cultural Change." In *Cultural Approach to History*, ed. Caroline Ware. New York: Columbia University Press.

Utterbach, James M. 1974. "Innovations in Industry and the Diffusion of Technology." *Science* 183:620–26.

Vasina, I. R., Maury Thomas, and L. V. Thomas. 1964. *The Historian in Tropical Africa*. London: Oxford University Press.

Vidal de la Blache, Paul M. J. 1926. *Principles of Human Geography*, trans. Millicent T. Bingham. New York: Holt.

Vital, David. 1967. *The Inequality of States: A Study of Small Power in International Relations*. Oxford: Clarendon.

Wagner, Philip. 1960. *The Human Uses of the Earth*. Glencoe, Ill.: Free Press.

Wallerstein, Immanuel. 1974. *The Modern World System*, vol. 1. New York: Academic.

Walters, Harry. 1975. "Difficult Issues Underlying Food Problems." *Science* 188:524–30.

Walton, John. 1979. "Urban Political Movements and Revolutionary Change in the Third World." *Urban Affairs Quarterly* 15:3–26.

Warner, Sam. 1966. "Innovation and the Industrialization of Philadelphia." In *The Historian and the City*, ed. Oscar Handlin and John Burchard. Cambridge: MIT Press.

Webb, Walter P. 1931. *The Great Plains*. New York: Grosset and Dunlap.

Webber, Melvin. 1963. "Order in Diversity: Community without Propinquity." In *Cities and Space: The Future of Urban Land*, ed. Lowden Wingo, Jr. Baltimore: Johns Hopkins University Press.

Weber, Max. 1922. *Wirtschaft und Gesellschaft*. Tubingen: Mohr.

Weinberg. Ian. 1969. "The Problem of Convergence of Industrial Societies: A Critical Look at the State of the Theory." *Comparative Studies in Society and History* 11:1–15.

Weiss, Paul A., ed. 1971. *Hierarchically Organized Systems in Theory and Practice*. New York: Hafner.

Wilkinson, Kenneth. 1970. "The Community as a Social Field." *Social Forces* 48: 311–21.

Wilkinson, Richard C. 1973. *Poverty and Progress: An Ecological Perspective on Economic Development*. New York: Praeger.

Williamson, Jeffrey. 1965. "Regional Inequality and the Process of National Development." *Economic Development and Cultural Change*, vol. 13, pt. 2.

Williamson, Oliver. 1980. "Emergence of the Visible Hand." In *Managerial Hierarchies: Comparative Perspectives on the Rise of Modern Enterprise*, ed. Alfred D. Chandler and Herman Daems. Cambridge: Harvard University Press.

Winsborough, Hal H. 1960. "Occupational Composition and the Urban Hierarchy." *American Sociological Review* 25:894–97.

Wolfe, Eric. 1957. "Closed Corporate Peasant Communities in Mesoamerica and Central Java." *Southwestern Journal of Anthropology* 13:1–18.

Wrigley, E. A. 1961. *Industrial Growth and Population Change*. Cambridge: Cambridge University Press.

Yearbook of International Organizations. 1984. Munich: K. G. Saur.

Zelinsky, Wilbur, and David F. Sly. 1984. "Personal Gasoline Consumption, Population Patterns, and Metropolitan Structure: The United States, 1960–1970." *Annals Association of American Geographers* 74:257–78.

Index

Abel, Theodore, 133
Abele, Lawrence G., 127
Abrahamse, Allan, 99
Abramowitz, M., 114
Adams, Robert McC., 14
Adaptation, 3, 4, 7, 8, 43
Adelman, Irma, 9
Aldrich, Howard, 78, 137
Allin, Bushrod W., 15
Anderson, Theodore, 78
Arrow, Kenneth, 28
Ashton, T. S., 120
Asymptote, 52, 57, 123
Auster, Ellen R., 78
Autecology, 1

Bailey, Kenneth D., 134
Baldridge, J. Victor, 48, 79
Barker, Roger, 11
Barnett, H. J., 111, 112
Barnum, Howard H., 9
Bendix, Rinehart, 84
Bennett, John W., 42
Benson, J., 82

Berry, Brian, 96, 126
Bertalanffy, Ludwig von, 53
Bidwell, Charles, 80
Binford, Lewis R., 64
Bioecology, 3, 126
Blau, Peter, 78
Boli-Bennett, John, 84
Bollen, Kenneth, 105
Boserup, Ester, 25
Boulding, Kenneth, 18, 28, 56, 115, 122, 136
Boundary: community, 89; ecosystem, 27, 103, 107; political, 102; regional, 94; temporal-spatial, 21
Bowen, Howard R., 114
Bradbury, Katherine, 129
Braidwood, Robert A., 14
Branscomb, Lewis M., 115
Braudel, Ferdinand, 48, 92
Brittain, Jack, 70, 80
Brooks, Harvey, 28
Brown, David, 140
Brown, Lester, 130